Fodor's
Waikiki

Rita and Jim Ariyoshi

Fodor's Travel Publications, Inc.
New York and London

Grateful acknowledgment is made to Davick Publications for permission to reprint "Diamond Head Inside Out" by Betty Fullard-Leo and "The Aloha Shirt" by DeSoto Brown from Aloha Magazine © Davick Publications. Reprinted with permission from Davick Publications.

Fodor's Waikiki

Editor: Jillian Magalaner
Editorial Contributors: Carmen Anthony, Anita Guerrini, Julia Lisella, Carolyn Price
Art Director: Fabrizio La Rocca
Cartographer: David Lindroth
Illustrator: Karl Tanner
Cover Photograph: Kishimoto/Uniphoto

Design: Vignelli Associates

About the Authors

Rita and Jim Ariyoshi live less than five minutes from Waikiki. Their award-winning stories and photographs have appeared in a wide variety of international publications including *Travel and Leisure*, *Islands*, and the *Los Angeles Times*. Rita is the author of the Hawaii best-seller, *Maui on My Mind*.

Special Sales

Fodor's Travel Publications are available at special discounts for bulk purchases (100 copies or more) for sales promotions or premiums. Special editions, including personalized covers, excerpts of existing guides, and corporate imprints, can be created in large quantities for special needs. For more information write to Special Marketing, Fodor's Travel Publications, 201 East 50th St., New York, NY 10022. Inquiries from the United Kingdom should be sent to Fodor's Travel Publications, 20 Vauxhall Bridge Rd., London, England SW1V 2SA.

MANUFACTURED IN THE UNITED STATES OF AMERICA

10 9 8 7 6 5 4 3 2 1

Contents

Foreword

We wish to express our gratitude to the Hawaii Visitors Bureau in Honolulu for their assistance in the preparation of this guidebook, especially to Lindy Boyes.

While every care has been taken to ensure the accuracy of the information in this guide, the passage of time will always bring change, and consequently, the publisher cannot accept responsibility for errors that may occur.

All prices and opening times quoted here are based on information supplied to us at press time. Hours and admission fees may change, however, and the prudent traveler will avoid inconvenience by calling ahead.

Fodor's wants to hear about your travel experiences, both pleasant and unpleasant. When a hotel or restaurant fails to live up to its billing, let us know and we will investigate the complaint and revise our entries where the facts warrant it.

Send your letters to the editors of Fodor's Travel Publications, 201 E. 50th Street, New York, NY 10022.

Highlights'91 and Fodor's Choice

Highlights '91

Waikiki has never looked better. The years of the massive multimillion-dollar renovation project are over. The sawhorses, jackhammers, and construction detours are gone, and so is the noise. Waikiki has settled back comfortably on its throne as the queen of tropical resorts.

Along the main street. Ten and a half million dollars has bought a new look for Kalakaua Avenue, making the famous main street that parallels the beach a grand thoroughfare. Sidewalks have been widened, traffic realigned, street signs improved, and clutter removed. Underfoot, earthtone tiles in tapalike Polynesian designs pave the sidewalks. Kiosks, benches, stately coconut palms, flowers, and festive night lighting all make Kalakaua Avenue a great place for strolling, day or night. New shops with well-known names add so much glitz and glamour that parts of Hawaii's most famous avenue are beginning to look a lot like Rodeo Drive in Beverly Hills. **Tiffany, Hermès, Chanel, Celine,** and **Gucci** are bringing designer chic to the land of grass skirts and flower leis.

The oldest hotel in town. The historic restoration of Waikiki's oldest hotel, the **Moana,** now regrettably called the **Sheraton Moana Surfrider,** is completed. The elegant Victorian grande dame of hotels, built in 1901, now looks like a magnificent white wedding cake among modern towers. There were very few compromises made in the Moana's restoration; Sheraton is to be commended for spending the money and going all the way with this one.

Sitting on the Moana's wide veranda during afternoon high tea, with a sandalwood fan (provided by the hotel), sipping something tall and cool with a wedge of pineapple on the glass rim, and listening to classical music while the tide rolls in is an experience to remember, a quiet moment packed with nostalgia for restful, more gracious days. In the morning, breakfast is served on the veranda, and there isn't a nicer spot in town. There are plans to serve Sunday brunch in the oceanside Grand Salon, and to present significant Hawaiiana programs beneath the spreading boughs of the huge banyan tree, where Robert Louis Stevenson once composed stories for the beautiful young Princess Kaiulani.

The hotel's Historical Room, in the rotunda overlooking the main entrance, displays old photographs, dance cards, menus (note the prices and weep), dishes, silverware, and other fascinating memorabilia, most of them sent to the Moana by former guests.

The room, the porches, and veranda are all open to the public and draw a steady crowd of local people hoping to recapture the Hawaii of a bygone era.

Waikiki's newest hotel. First it was supposed to open in 1989 and they were calling it the Waikiki Prince. Now it's scheduled to open practically any minute as we go to press, and its new name is the **Hawaii Prince Hotel.** With 521 rooms in two tall towers, this may very well be Waikiki's last big hotel, because the resort has simply run out of room. Built at a cost of $150 million, the luxury property overlooks the Ala Wai Yacht Harbor and will have five restaurants and a grand ballroom. If the food is anything like the cuisine at the Maui Prince at Makena (and the owners say it will be), the restaurants will be a very welcome addition to Waikiki's inventory of fine dining establishments. Included in the five will be the hotel's signature dining room, the Prince Court, and the Hakone, a copy of the Maui Prince's classic Kyoto-style Japanese restaurant.

The whaling wall goes extinct. The 20-story mural painted on the side of the Waikiki Marina condominium, right at the entrance to Waikiki, is almost totally obscured by the construction of the Hawaii Prince Hotel. At press time, the last of the great humpbacks is diving into a metal scaffolding. Controversial from the day the artist shot the first blast of paint from his spray gun on Christmas Day in 1984, the half-acre painting is about to become just another whopper of a fish story. A few traces may still be there, to give an idea of the scope of the mural.

The biggest resort on the island. About $100 million has already been spent on the **Hilton Hawaiian Village** for renovations and additions, and they're still spending and adding. The latest word is that the hotel will be developing a complete health-spa complex including tennis courts and a gourmet health-food restaurant.

The Golden Dragon, the hotel's premier Chinese restaurant, has moved to the Rainbow Tower overlooking the lagoon, and has a romantic outdoor dining area. In addition to serving the best Chinese food in Honolulu, with such dishes as Imperial Beggar's Chicken (wrapped in lotus leaves and baked in clay, and requiring 24 hours' notice), the restaurant has a restrained and sophisticated decor radiating a serene, Asian ambience. The serving staff includes Sylon the Tea Lady, star of a little tea drama enacted at each table. She also tells fortunes at no extra charge.

More village entertainment. It's new, it's one of the best pageants in Waikiki, and it's free. Every Friday evening the Hilton Hawaiian Village stages its King Kalakaua Jubilee, poolside, with the beach as a backdrop. It's a monarchy-era musical presentation with pomp, song, hula, a fire swallower, and painless history, culminating in a spectacular fireworks show.

Waikiki's newest dinner show. This one's at the Hilton Hawaiian Village, too. Charo, the coochie-coochie girl, is wowing them at the hotel's Tropic's Surf Club. If you add up her years in show business, it would indicate that Charo is no spring chicken, but she still has the face and body of a tee-nybopper and she prances her way through a high-energy salsa performance in drop-dead costumes. The buffet dinner is pretty good, too. Charo joins Hilton's star lineup consisting of the legendary Don Ho and his Polynesian extravaganza at the Village Dome Showroom, jazzman Jimmy Borges playing Gershwin, Cole Porter, and Jerome Kern dance tunes in the Paradise Lounge, and a host of other top Hawaiian entertainers at the hotel's various bars and lounges.

Sushi in Surferland. Located on the North Shore of Oahu (legendary for its winter waves and championship surfing competitions) the Turtle Bay Hilton has introduced the area's first Japanese restaurant, **Asahi.** Select from 50 kinds of sushi, or choose tempura or teriyaki. The hotel has also just expanded its Sunday brunch to include a waffle bar and taco bar. The floor-to-ceiling windows in the Sea Tide Room look out on surfers riding those fabulous waves.

Book a boutique. Mega-resorts may be the mega-trend, but small boutique hotels are continuing to spring up in Waiki-ki, offering intimate, personalized alternatives. First, in 1988, came the **Waikiki Joy,** placing an emphasis on high-tech amenities, followed by the **Coconut Plaza** with its chic decor and low rates.

A sinking feeling. Atlantis Submarines, operating for years in the Caribbean, now has a 65-foot, 80-ton sub going down off Waikiki. It carries up to 46 passengers in comfortable seats, each facing a big viewing porthole, and dives to a depth of 100 feet. This is a real sub that really dives, not a Disney thrill ride. The Atlantis people, working in coopera-tion with the University of Hawaii, have sunk a 174-foot ship, constructed an artificial reef at the dive site, and plan to sink an airplane. The underwater attractions have drawn schools of colorful reef fish which are fed leftovers from the Hilton's champagne breakfast by Atlantis scuba divers. It's quite a sight. The really sad aspect of the experience is the knowledge that the fish that were once so naturally bounti-ful in the area have been depleted by the foreign drift-net fishermen operating in Hawaiian waters in the past few years. The ocean floor just feet away from the feeding sight is a desert. Included in the Atlantis dive fee is a catamaran ride to the dive site, and a sailing tour of the Waikiki and Diamond Head shoreline.

A new high. Aloha IslandAir, the commuter arm of the interisland giant, **Aloha Airlines,** has initiated one-day flightseeing tours of Oahu, Molokai, Lanai, Maui, Kahoola-we, and the Big Island aboard a specially equipped de Havilland Dash-6 aircraft with excellent viewing windows and individual headsets. The tour includes Hawaii Volca-noes National Park, on the Big Island; Maui's Haleakala

Crater; a visit to the 225,000-acre Parker Ranch, the largest privately owned ranch in the United States, located on the Big Island; a 2½-hour stop in Lahaina, Maui's historical whaling town; and a visit to Kalaupapa Peninsula on Molokai, where Father Damien labored among the victims of Hansen's disease (leprosy). The site, at the foot of Molokai's sea cliffs, which are the tallest in the world, is now an incredibly beautiful and emotionally moving national park. The tour departs daily from Honolulu and includes pickup in Waikiki, lunch in Lahaina, and a color photograph.

A big new resort on Oahu. The sunny forecast for Hawaii's tourism industry and lack of room for expansion in Waikiki have encouraged the construction of **Ko Olina,** a vast $3 billion resort along the dry Ewa Coast west of Honolulu International Airport. It will include seven hotels having a total of 4,000 rooms, 5,200 condominium units, a 44-acre marina, its own 18-hole golf course, a tennis complex, and a shopping center. Situated on 642 acres, it will be the state's largest resort. Some 3,000 coconut palms have already been planted. Among the hotels will be the **Pan Pacific, Loew's,** and the **Four Seasons.** A luxury seaside condo named the **Royal Ko Olina** will have 320 luxury units complete with limousine and pantry services and a health club.

A whole new city on Oahu. Also slated for the West Beach area is a "second city" to absorb Hawaii's phenomenal growth. It will have single-family homes, condominiums, and a business district.

Cheering up Chinatown. The area had long languished in the shadow of Honolulu's downtown skyscrapers, almost forgotten, pursuing its fragrant (the smells of incense, fish, and flowers mingling), mysterious lifestyle, slightly tawdry, a little rickety, but always fascinating. Now a renaissance has drawn artists, smart galleries, and little restaurants to the area where they reside among the lei stands, noodle shops, and herbalists. It's suddenly chic to have a shop in Chinatown.

Food news. Led by a bright, young group of talented European and American chefs, Hawaii is developing its own distinctive regional cuisine, using the area's unique produce and combining aspects of classical French and California nouvelle with the traditional cooking styles of Asia. After several attempts at naming the trend, foodies seem to have adopted "Pacific Rim Cuisine" as the most descriptive term. The new cuisine has been earning national attention, and some of the best places to sample it are right in Waikiki.

Getting off the ground. Because of the vagaries of airport construction, the **Pacific Aerospace Museum,** which is said to have cost $2 million, still has not opened at Honolulu International Airport. When it is finally launched (no firm date was set at press time), it will have a multimedia theater which will allow visitors to stand seemingly on the deck of a space shuttle, witness the infamous attack on Pearl Harbor, and fly into the airport itself.

The Convention Center controversy continues. Honolulu has needed a major convention facility for a long time. The big question has been where to put it. In its 1988 session, the Hawaii State Legislature chose the International Market Place as the site, leaving many segments of the travel industry aghast at the decision to place the convention center in the heart of already crowded Waikiki—and wipe out a popular tourist attraction at the same time. The options are still open, however, because another site just outside Waikiki near Ala Moana Shopping Center, has just been approved for development by First Development, Inc., of Tokyo. The complex will include a 500-foot hotel tower and two 450-foot condominium towers. They will be Hawaii's tallest buildings. Provided the project doesn't run into government snags, Honolulu may end up with two convention centers: The Tokyo-financed International Market Place, slated to cost over a billion dollars, will be completed sometime in 1994.

Sighs of the times. The Kodak Hula Show, which has offered free performances in Waikiki for 50 years, is now charging an admission fee of $2.50. A Kodak spokesman said the charge is necessary to defray mounting costs; any profits will be donated to charity.

At press time, the new **Hawaii Children's Museum** was scheduled to open in the revamped Dole Pineapple Cannery, renamed Dole Cannery Square. The focus of the new museum will be "You, the Child."

Fodor's Choice

No two people will agree on what makes a perfect vacation, but it's fun and helpful to know what others think. We hope you'll have a chance to experience some of Fodor's Choices yourself while visiting Waikiki. For detailed information about each entry, refer to the appropriate chapters in this guidebook.

Beaches

Bellows Beach on the weekends

Kailua Beach

Sans Souci Beach

Waikiki in front of the Hyatt Regency Hotel

Waikiki in front of the Royal Hawaiian Hotel

Waimea Bay in summer (it can be extremely dangerous in winter)

Best Buys

Aloha shirts—Andrade for quality; outlets and street stalls for price

Ethnic finds—Mandalay, Kitamura's

Fine jewelry—Haimoff & Haimoff

Funky fashion—Chocolates for Breakfast for women, Altillo for men

Hawaiian arts and crafts—Little Hawaiian Craft Shop

Most fun—Shirokiya

Muumuus—Liberty House stores

Variety—Ala Moana Shopping Center

Drives

From Hawaii Kai to Waimanalo

Likelike Highway on the windward side

Pali Highway

Festivals

Aloha Week Festival

Kamehameha Day

Lei Day

For Kids

Honolulu Zoo, especially the giraffe tower

Oceanarium Restaurant, Pacific Beach Hotel

Sea Life Park

Surfing lessons, Waikiki Beach

Waikiki Aquarium

Golf Courses

Olomana Golf Links, public

Waialae Country Club, if you know a member

Hotels

Colony Surf *(Very Expensive)*

Halekulani *(Very Expensive)*

Hyatt Regency Waikiki *(Very Expensive)*

Kahala Hilton *(Very Expensive)*

Royal Hawaiian *(Very Expensive)*

Hilton Hawaiian Village *(Expensive)*

Waikiki Joy *(Expensive)*

Aston Waikikian on the Beach *(Moderate)*

Coconut Plaza *(Moderate)*

Kamaaina (Islanders') Favorites

Manapua (a steamed bun with sweet pork filling) from any lunch wagon at Sandy Beach

Poi lunch at The Willows

Shave ice with vanilla ice cream and *azuki* beans at Aoki's in Haleiwa

Sunday brunch at the Halekulani

Sunset picnic at Queen's Beach

Luau

Royal Hawaiian Hotel

Local Dishes

Any local seafood, especially opakapaka

Laulau

Lomilomi salmon

Macadamia nut cream pie at the Willows

Manapua

Mango anything, in season

Passion-orange juice

"Plate lunch" from one of the beach lunch wagons—not gourmet, but an experience

Poha jam

Saimin (noodle soup that might include shrimp, green onion, fish cake, and pork)

Nightlife

The Black Orchid

Danny Kaleikini Show, Kahala Hilton

Nicholas Nickolas

Nick's Fishmarket

Polynesian Cultural Center Evening Show

Trappers, Hyatt Regency Waikiki

Restaurants

Bagwells 2424, Hyatt Regency Hotel *(Very Expensive)*

Kamaaina Suite, The Willows *(Very Expensive)*

La Mer, Halekulani Hotel *(Very Expensive)*

Best Japanese—Kacho, Waikiki Parc Hotel *(Expensive)*

Best Seafood—Nick's Fishmarket *(Expensive)*

Baci *(Moderate)*

Best Chinese—Golden Dragon, Hilton Hawaiian Village *(Moderate)*

Bon Appetit *(Moderate)*

Orchids, Halekulani Hotel *(Moderate)*

Romantic Hideaways

Breakfast at Michel's at the Colony Surf

Dinner at The Secret

Lunch at the Tahitian Lanai

Picnic at the Waikiki Shell

Room in the old section of the Royal Hawaiian Hotel

Sights

Arizona Memorial

Byodo-In Temple

Polynesian Cultural Center

Sea Life Park

Sunsets

Diamond Head Lighthouse

Sunset Beach, North Shore

Waikiki Beach

Views

Makapuu Point

Nuuanu Pali Lookout

Top of the Ilikai Waikiki Hotel

Upper ocean-view rooms at the Sheraton Waikiki and Halekulani hotels

Honolulu Including Waikiki

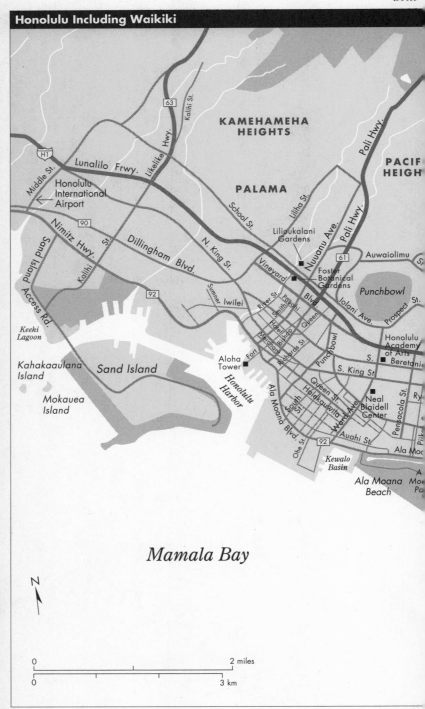

KAMEHAMEHA
HEIGHTS

PACIFIC
HEIGHTS

Lunalilo Frwy.

Honolulu
International
Airport

PALAMA

Middle St.

H1

63

Likelike Hwy.

Kalihi St.

Pali Hwy.

School St.

Liliha St.

Nuuanu Ave.

Nimitz Hwy.

90

Kalihi St.

Dillingham Blvd.

N. King St.

Vineyard

Lilioukalani
Gardens

61

Auwaiolimu

Pali Hwy.

Sand Island Access Rd.

92

Summer St.

Iwilei

River St.

Pauahi

Smith

Vineyard Blvd.

Foster
Botanical
Gardens

Iolani Ave.

Prospect St.

Punchbowl

Keehi
Lagoon

Kahakaaulana
Island

Sand Island

Mokauea
Island

Aloha
Tower

Honolulu
Harbor

Fort

Merchant

Hotel

Bishop

Bethel

Richards St.

Queen

Punchbowl

S. Beretania

S. King St

Honolulu
Academy
of Arts

Ala Moana Blvd.

South St.

Queen St.

Halekauwila

Ward Ave.

Neal
Blaidell
Center

Pensacola St.

Piikoi

92

Auahi St.

Ohe St.

Kewalo
Basin

Ala Moana

Ala Moana
Beach

Ala
Moana
Park

Mamala Bay

N

0   2 miles

0   3 km

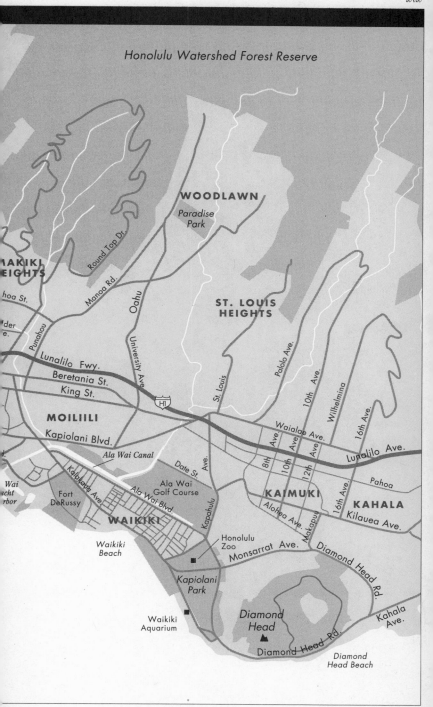

Honolulu Watershed Forest Reserve

WOODLAWN

Paradise
Park

MAKIKI
HEIGHTS

ST. LOUIS
HEIGHTS

Round Top Dr.

Manoa Rd.

Oahu

hoa St.

der
e.

Punahou

University Ave.

Lunalilo Fwy.

Beretania St.

King St.

St. Louis

Palolo Ave.

10th Ave.

Wilhelmina

16th Ave.

H1

MOILIILI

Kapiolani Blvd.

Waialae Ave.

Lunalilo Ave.

Ala Wai Canal

Date St.

Ave.

Ave.

8th
Ave.

10th
Ave.

12th
Ave.

Pahoa

Wai
cht
rbor

Kalakaua Ave.

Fort
DeRussy

Ala Wai
Golf Course

Ala Wai Blvd.

Kapahulu

KAIMUKI

Alohea Ave.

Makapuu

16th Ave.

KAHALA

Kilauea Ave.

WAIKIKI

Honolulu
Zoo

Monsarrat Ave.

Diamond Head Rd.

Waikiki
Beach

Kapiolani
Park

Kahala
Ave.

Waikiki
Aquarium

Diamond
Head

Diamond Head Rd.

Diamond
Head Beach

World Time Zones

Numbers below vertical bands relate each zone to Greenwich Mean Time (0 hrs.).
Local times frequently differ from these general indications,
as indicated by light-face numbers on map.

Algiers, **29**
Anchorage, **3**
Athens, **41**
Auckland, **1**
Baghdad, **46**
Bangkok, **50**
Beijing, **54**

Berlin, **34**
Bogotá, **19**
Budapest, **37**
Buenos Aires, **24**
Caracas, **22**
Chicago, **9**
Copenhagen, **33**
Dallas, **10**

Delhi, **48**
Denver, **8**
Djakarta, **53**
Dublin, **26**
Edmonton, **7**
Hong Kong, **56**
Honolulu, **2**

Istanbul, **40**
Jerusalem, **42**
Johannesburg, **44**
Lima, **20**
Lisbon, **28**
London (Greenwich), **27**
Los Angeles, **6**
Madrid, **38**
Manila, **57**

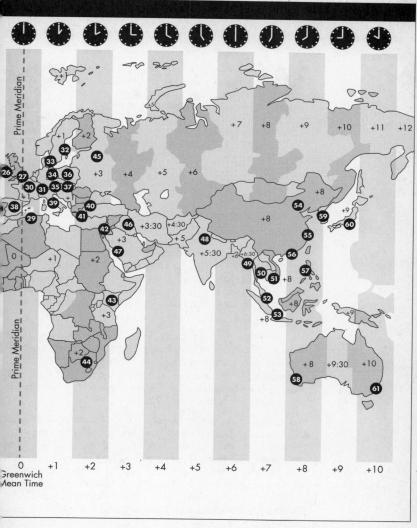

+1 +2 +3 +4 +5 +6 +7 +8 +9 +10 +11 +12

Prime Meridian

Prime Meridian

0 +1 +2 +3 +4 +5 +6 +7 +8 +9 +10

Greenwich
Mean Time

+3:30 +4:30 +5 +5:30 +6 +6:30 +8 +9 +9:30 +10

Introduction

Waikiki—the very word conjures images as diverse as dreams. Some people think of a full moon sailing over Diamond Head, while silver-crested waves sweep toward a sandy shore. For others, Waikiki is Surf City—free, easy, and loud, a youth hangout in Paradise. Television fans recall Jack Lord on *Hawaii Five-O* snapping, "Book 'em, Dano," and *Magnum, P.I.'s* Tom Selleck racing down the main drag in his red Ferrari. And let's face it, for some people, Waikiki means a tacky tourist trap and crass commercialism. All of it is true and yet, none is entirely true.

There are a lot of misconceptions about Waikiki, some of them promoted by the people who market this international resort. They still cite Robert Louis Stevenson, who wrote in his hotel register when checking out in 1893, "If anyone desires such old-fashioned things as lovely scenery, quiet, pure air, clear sea water, good food, and heavenly sunsets hung out before his eyes over the Pacific and the distant hills of Waianae, I recommend him cordially to the Sans Souci."

Almost a hundred years later, Waikiki has come of age. It is no longer a languid tropical outpost, but a sophisticated resort city on the order of Rio de Janeiro or Hong Kong. Sure, Stevenson's scenery is just as lovely, the sunsets are sheer poetry, the ocean is clear, the air is pure, and the food is better than ever. But quiet? No way.

Waikiki has more action packed within its perimeters than all the rest of Hawaii combined. Bordered by the ocean on the south, it sparkles along 2½ miles of spangled sea from the famous Diamond Head landmark on the east to the Ala Wai Yacht Harbor on the west. Separated from the sprawling city of Honolulu by the broad Ala Wai Canal on its northern boundary, Waikiki is 3½ miles from downtown Honolulu and worlds apart from any other city in the world. Nowhere else is there such a salad of cultures so artfully tossed, each one retaining its distinct flavor and texture. McDonald's offers burgers and *saimin*, the ubiquitous noodle soup of Nippon. You'll find yourself saying things like *aloha* and *mahalo* (thank you). You'll find almost as many sushi bars as ice cream stands.

More than 3 million visitors a year now sleep in the more than 34,000 rooms of the 174 resort properties tucked into 1.5 square miles of Pacific playground. They come from every point of the compass. Waikiki vibrates with international excitement and offers more to see, do, and eat than all the other Hawaiian islands combined.

Take the nightlife. If you were a mega star, wouldn't you want to book a few days in Hawaii on your world tour? Most do. There's also a good crop of local talent, ranging from the old pro Don Ho and his Vegas-style hula show to luaus on the beach, video discos, and old-fashioned cheek-to-cheek dancing beneath the palms at the Royal Hawaiian Hotel. The cabarets don't close till 4 AM.

Hawaii is the cultural and commercial crossroads of the Pacific, and Waikiki is its economic base. Waikiki is where most of the 6 million tourists a year spend at least a few nights. Because of these factors, the shops in Waikiki are bursting with the wares of the world, everything from Australian sheepskins to Oriental jade to Paris designer fashions. You can choose between a vulgar ashtray or a magnificent handcrafted rug from mainland China. Women can outfit themselves in a basic black Chanel dress or a neon-orange muumuu, while the men can pick a brazen aloha shirt or an imported Mondo Tallia suit. In between the two extremes, beautifully made resort wear is setting the pace in the lucrative world of fashion.

Dining has come to be one of the great Waikiki experiences. That wasn't true five years ago—maybe not even three. But with success has come a new commitment to excellence in cuisine, particularly at the big hotels. You'll find cordon bleu chefs, and veterans of Maxim's in Paris and the Four Seasons in New York. These chefs are now whipping up wok dishes with a French flair, wrapping taro and local lobster in phyllo pastry, and creating new culinary delights with passion fruit. The food of Hawaii, heavily influenced by its multicultural heritage, has been combined with traditional schools of cooking, giving birth to a new regional cuisine. Of course, there's still meat and potatoes, fish, and poi aplenty, along with a bounty of moderately priced restaurants and a glut of snack bars, budget eateries, all-you-can-eat buffets, and brand-name burgers. To spice the pot, there's Thai, Greek, Korean, Indian, French, German, Mexican, and Italian food. In all, the restaurants number 240, just in Waikiki.

Even with all these attractions, the star of Waikiki is still the beach—that 2½-mile strand of golden sand, anchored on one end by familiar, beloved, cliché-ridden Diamond Head, and melting into golden sunsets beyond the Ala Wai Yacht Harbor on the other. Fringed by palms and festooned with glittering hotels, it is easily one of the best swimming beaches in the world, gentle with a good sandy bottom, clean and sparkling.

I happen to be a fan of Waikiki. I'm part of a growing number of local residents who have discovered that you don't have to go half a world away for a brief vacation. We choose Waikiki for romantic weekends, we bring the children on Saturdays, we picnic, we go to the zoo and the aquarium—

and we swim at what many of us consider the world's greatest beach.

Waikiki has a special quality to it that sets it apart from other places. Couples who probably haven't held hands in 20 years touch tenderly like schoolchildren—there he is in his brown shoes and walking shorts and she with a flower in her gray hair. Honeymooners from Japan laugh shyly, playing in the surf, and servicemen clown on aqua bikes. There's the glory of a first surfing lesson, when you actually stand up and ride a wave, girls with their hair streaming behind them and grins lighting their faces, boys affecting a casual stance—the California hot-dawg look. Everyone is really having fun.

Most of Hawaii's visitors have been here before. That says a lot when there are other sunny places in the world, and many are a lot closer to home and cheaper.

I still think of my own first morning in Waikiki, awakening to the sound of the surf right outside my window (a few floors down, of course, but it sounded as if it was about to dampen everything but my spirits). I could hear the tinkle of crystal, and, peeking out the window, I saw ladies robed in flowered muumuus setting the tables for breakfast, with pink cloths and china, on the edge of the beach. Early swimmers were already in the sea, and intrepid surfers were riding the morning waves. Diamond Head was still in shadow. I was enchanted.

One of the impressive things about Waikiki is the manner in which people are treated. We've all traveled, and we know the difference between being treated well and being treated rudely. And let's face it, we often judge a whole country, a whole group of people, by the actions of a few. Let a taxi driver snap at us—and we won't return. Let one man go out of his way to show us the right road, and we wax euphoric about how friendly and warm the people are.

Whether it's the stark realization that tourism is Hawaii's number one business, accounting for one out of every three dollars of the state's revenue, or whether it's the Hawaiian tradition of hospitality, the visitor is king. He or she is treated with kindness and welcomed with a sincere warmth. I think the welcome is part good business and part the real spirit of aloha that still pervades every aspect of Hawaiian life. Probably it is this spirit, as much as the postcard beauty of the place, that sets Waikiki apart.

Waikiki is only one glittering part of the cosmopolitan city of Honolulu, America's only city with a royal past. The business pace is brisk, yet the people flit among the skyscrapers in flowing muumuus and bright aloha shirts. There are tree-shaded parks, temples that look like they were transported intact from the Orient, and impressive examples of the arts, from opera and French impressionist paintings to kabuki and the Japanese tea ceremony.

The residents live in towering condominiums in the suburbs or in little white houses tucked deep in the valleys. There are no slums, although portions of downtown look like a seedy, tattered seaport catering to the fleets of the world. The wonderful old buildings of the area are beginning to attract artists and gallery owners and a few good restaurateurs who are willing to brave the tawdriness in exchange for great space at low rent. They ignite the blighted blocks with smart mauve-and-alabaster-tone windows.

With the cost of living here being the second highest in the nation, most Honolulu men and women work. These workers eat at more fast-food restaurants per capita than in most places and are subjected to choked freeways during rush hour. Still, most Honolulans wouldn't trade their city for any other. Most of them can be at the beach in minutes, and going out for an evening of dinner and the theater is not a major project. The distances are manageable.

Honolulu is located on the island of Oahu, which encompasses only 608 square miles. Even though Honolulu is the capital of Hawaii, and 80% of the state's population resides on Oahu, the island remains surprisingly unspoiled and rural. There are miles of uncrowded beaches. More than 50 beach parks with rest rooms, showers, and picnic tables are sprinkled along the shoreline—and that's not counting the places where you can just pull off to the side of the road and picnic or swim. Each beach is known for a different ocean activity, such as snorkeling, bodysurfing, swimming, and windsurfing.

The center of the island is carpeted in pineapple plantations. Acres of waving sugarcane go down almost to the sea. There are ranches, banana farms, and fields of exotic flowers grown for export. The plantation towns are small. Some have become cute with boutiques and little art galleries. Others are just themselves—old, wooden, and picturesque —the small homes surrounded by a riot of flowers and trees heavy with mango, pomelo, and ychee.

Oahu's mountain vistas are among the most beautiful this planet has to offer. The island was formed by two volcanoes that, with the help of erosion, became two mountain ranges —the western Waianae Mountains, rising 4,000 feet above sea level, and the eastern Koolaus, more than 3,000 verdant feet high, right in back of Waikiki.

All the Hawaiian Islands are volcanic in origin, formed over the eons by submarine eruptions that built the islands one by one. The action of wind, rain, and water has sculpted jagged peaks, deep valleys, and sheer green cliffs. The rise and fall of the ocean and the creation of coral shelves resulted in the two great harbors, Honolulu and Pearl, that determined Oahu's destiny as a Pacific capital.

Hawaii's kings and queens ruled from the Iolani Palace in downtown Honolulu, and it was at Iolani where the American flag first flew over the Islands. Even in those days of royalty, the virtues of Waikiki as a playground were noticed. Long processions of *alii* (nobility) would make their way across the streams and swamps, past the duck ponds, to the coconut groves and the beach. King David Kalakaua had a boat house in Waikiki, and the lovely Princess Kaiulani had a home there.

By the 1880s, guest houses were sprinkled along the beach like confetti. The first hotel, the Moana, was built at the turn of the century. At that time, Waikiki was connected to the rest of Honolulu by a tram, bringing townspeople to the shore. In 1927, the "Pink Palace of the Pacific," the Royal Hawaiian Hotel, was built by Matson Navigation Company to accommodate travelers arriving on luxury liners. It was opened with a grand ball, and Waikiki was launched as a first-class tourist destination, duck ponds, taro patches, and all. The rich and famous came from around the world. December 7, 1941, brought that era to a close, with the bombing of Pearl Harbor and Hawaii's entry into the war in the Pacific. The Royal Hawaiian was turned over to American servicemen. Hundreds of war-weary soldiers and sailors found a warm welcome in Waikiki.

With victory came the boom. By 1952, Waikiki had 2,000 hotel rooms. In 1969, there were 15,000 rooms. Today, that figure has more than doubled.

Waikiki sits on the sunny dry side of Oahu, one of the eight major Hawaiian islands, seven of which are inhabited. In all, there are 132 Hawaiian isles and atolls, stretched across 1,600 miles of ocean. Hawaii is America's most exotic, most unusual state, and Waikiki is its generator, keeping everything humming. It incorporates all the natural splendors of the Islands and synthesizes them with elegance and daring into an international resort city in the middle of the vast blue Pacific.

1 Essential Information

Before You Go

Visitor Information

A trip is a considerable investment in both time and money, and it's hard to say which is more precious these days. A travel agent who has been to Hawaii can help you cut through a lot of the details. He or she will also know most of the airline packages and special tours.

Most travel agents work on a commission from the airlines, hotels, and attractions. You pay no more—and often less—than if you made your arrangements on your own.

The source of all information on Hawaii is the **Hawaii Visitors Bureau** (HVB). The bureau's main office is located right in Waikiki (2270 Kalakaua Ave., 8th floor, Honolulu, 96815, tel. 808/923-1811).

HVB is a sophisticated communications network attuned to the needs of the visitor, and consumer oriented. The bureau publishes three free booklets. The *Calendar of Events* lists all the special holidays and annual festivals. Just give the staff your arrival date and they'll mail the appropriate booklet. The bureau also publishes an *Accommodation Guide*, which lists the various lodging choices in Hawaii in every price range. The guide tells you how close an accommodation is to the beach, and whether it has a pool and such amenities as refrigerators and televisions. The third is a *Restaurant Guide*, listing the 560 HVB-member restaurants in the state, each with a one-line description and a price category. There are no rating systems in the guides, just the bare facts.

The bureau also maintains offices on the Mainland:

New York: 441 Lexington Ave., Room 1407, NY 10017, tel. 212/986-9203.
Los Angeles: 3440 Wilshire Blvd., CA 90010, tel. 213/385-5301.
Chicago: 180 N. Michigan Ave., Suite 1031, IL 60601, tel. 312/236-0632.
San Francisco: 50 California St., CA 94111, tel. 415/392-8173.

HVB Meetings and Conventions office:

Washington, DC: 1511 K St. NW, Suite 415, DC 20005, tel. 202/393-6752.

Regional offices:

Canada: 4915 Cedar Crescent, Delta, B.C., Canada, V4M 1J9, tel. 604/943-8555.
Great Britain: 2 Cinnamon Row, Plantation Wharf, York Pl., London SW11 3TW, tel. 071/924-3999.
Japan: 129 Kokusai Bldg., 1-1, 3-chome, Maruno-uchi, Chiyoda-ku, Tokyo, Japan 100, tel. 03/287-2651 or 2652.

Tour Groups

Like most things in the Islands, package tours are a bit more laid-back than in other parts of the world. They usually include airfare, accommodations, transfers, some sightseeing, and plenty of free time to put some sand between your toes. Choosing a tour often comes down to how inclusive you want it to be:

Do you want to know all your meals are paid for before you leave, or would you rather hunt out the local eatery? Would you prefer to arrange a private sail, or is a group outing on a catamaran fine with you? Both preferences are easily accommodated.

When considering a tour, be sure to find out exactly what expenses are included (particularly tips, taxes, side trips, additional meals, and entertainment), ratings of all hotels on the itinerary and the facilities they offer, cancellation policies for both you and the tour operator, and the cost of the single supplement if you are traveling alone. Most tour operators request that bookings be made through a travel agent; there is no additional charge for doing so.

General-Interest Tours

Maupintour (Box 807, Lawrence, KA 66044, tel. 913/843–1211 or 800/255–4266) offers tours to Oahu teamed with the other islands. A 13-day trip to all four islands includes helicopter "flightseeing." **American Express Vacations** (Box 5014, Atlanta, GA 30302, tel. 800/241–1700 or in Georgia, 800/282–0800) is a veritable supermarket of tours. **Pleasant Hawaiian Holidays** (2404 Townsgate Rd., Box 5020, Westlake Village, CA 91359, tel. 818/991–3390 or 800/242–9244) also offers tours by the cartful, including low-priced packages for short visits. **Talmage Tours** (1223 Walnut St., Philadelphia, PA 19107, tel. 215/923–7100) has a nine-day Waikiki and Kauai package. Other major operators include **Cartan Tours** (12755 Hwy. 55, Suite 101, Minneapolis, MN 55441, tel. 612/540–8999) and **Island Holidays Tours** (2255 Kuhio Ave., Box 8519, Honolulu, HI 96815, tel. 808/945–6000).

British Tour Operators

Albany Travel (Manchester) Ltd. Central Bldgs., 211 Deansgate, Manchester M3 3NW, tel. 061/83–0202) offers seven nights at Waikiki Beach from £738 to £1,215 per person or 14 nights from £843 to £1,796. It also has self-catering vacations.

Hawaiian Holidays Tours, Inc. (308 Regent St., London W1R 5AL, tel. 071/580–9998/9), is the only Hawaiian company directly available to the European market, and all its prices are quoted in dollars. A three-night stay in Waikiki ranges from $128 to $566 per person in a twin room. Seven nights in a condominium costs from $638 for two people. It also offers escorted tours to Waikiki, Maui, and Kauai, with prices starting from $1,045. Round-trip airfares from London to Honolulu are *not* included.

Jetsave (Sussex House, London Rd., East Grinstead, West Sussex RH19 1LD, tel. 0342/328231) offers seven nights at Waikiki Beach from £705 to £865 per person or 14 nights from £795 to £959.

Poundstretcher (Airlink House, Hazlewick Ave., Three Bridges, Crawley, West Sussex RH10 1YS, tel. 0293/518022) offers hotel vacations for seven nights from £685, or at a holiday village with prices for seven nights from £835 and 14 nights from £1,099. It also offers two other vacations: Waikiki and Maui for 14 nights from £899 or Waikiki and Kauai for 14 nights from £965.

Package Deals for Independent Travelers

Liberty Travel/Gogo Tours (50 A & S Dr., Paramus, NJ 07652, tel. 201/967–3000) has packages ranging from 2 to 16 days with options for sightseeing and discounted car rental. **American Express**'s 50-page Hawaii brochure has a wide selection of independent packages. **Classic Hawaii** (65 W. Santa Clara St., San Jose, CA 95113, tel. 405/287–9101 or 800/221–3949) has packages featuring upscale hotels and resorts. Also check with **Delta Airlines** (tel. 800/221–6666 or 404/765–2952), **United Airlines** (tel. 800/328– 6877 or 312/952–4000), **American Fly Away Vacations** (tel. 800/433–7300 or 817/355–1234), and **Continental Airlines** (tel. 713/821–2100).

Passports, Visas, and Customs

Travel Documents Persons who are not citizens of the United States require a passport and a visa. Canadians only need to prove their place of birth with a passport, birth certificate, or similar document. British travelers will need a valid, 10-year passport (cost £15) and a U.S. Visitor's Visa, which you can get either through your travel agent or by post from the **United States Embassy, Visa and Immigration Dept.** (5 Upper Grosvenor St., London W1A 2JB, tel. 071/499-3443 recorded message, or 499–7010). The embassy no longer accepts visa applications made by personal callers. No vaccinations are required.

Restrictions on Import and Export Plants and plant products are subject to control by the Department of Agriculture, both on entering and leaving Hawaii. Pineapples and coconuts pass freely; avocados, bananas, lychees, and papayas must be treated. All other fruits are banned for export to the U.S. mainland. Flowers pass except for gardenia, rose, jade vine, and mauna loa. Seeds, except in leis and jewelry, are banned. Also banned are insects, snails, coffee, cotton, cacti, sugarcane, all berries, and soil.

Customs for British Travelers If you are 21 or over, you may take in 200 cigarettes or 50 cigars or 2 kilograms of tobacco; one liter of alcohol; and duty-free gifts to a value of $100. Be careful not to try to take in meat or meat products, seeds, plants, or fruits. Avoid illegal drugs like the plague.

Returning to the United Kingdom, you may take home, if you are 17 and over: (1) 200 cigarettes or 100 cigarillos or 50 cigars or 250 grams of tobacco; (2) two liters of table wine and (a) one liter of alcohol over 22% by volume (most spirits), or (b) two liters of alcohol under 22% by volume (fortified or sparkling wine), (3) 60 milliliters of perfume and ¼ liter of toilet water; and (4) other goods up to a value of £32.

Pets Leave dogs and other pets at home. A strict 120-day quarantine is imposed to keep out rabies, which is nonexistent in Hawaii. For full details, write to the **Animal Quarantine Station, Department of Agriculture,** State of Hawaii, 99–770 Moanalua Rd., Aiea, HI 96701.

When to Go

Hawaii has been called the land of eternal June. Blessed with sunshine and cooled by trade winds, it has one of the most ideal climates in the world. Situated well within the tropics, at latitude 20, Waikiki's year-round temperatures are mild, with a comfortable average of 75–80 degrees F (23–25 degrees C). The tropical location also means that there's little variation in the amount of daylight whether in June or December. The shortest day is 11 hours and the longest, 13½. When day finally surrenders to night, the sun goes down off Waikiki in a blaze of glory, painting the sky and ocean in passionate vermilion, scarlet, and gold. A fleet of pleasure boats waits to take you out to sea on sunset cruises with music and dancing. It's just as dramatic watching from the sand, as the sun silhouettes the volcanic Waianae Mountains and the surfers ride waves tinged with gold.

With such a consistently good climate, Waikiki's peak tourist seasons have more to do with the weather elsewhere. Pale hordes with parkas over their arms arrive in mid-December, and the crowds don't thin until April. Room rates run 10%–15% higher during this period than during the rest of the year. Summer, during the school vacation, is another crowded time for Waikiki, when families and young people gather, but the rates don't rise then as they do in winter.

Stretched out along the dry leeward shore, Waikiki rarely has two or three days of rain in a row. If it does rain, it will probably do so in February or March, when the prevailing northeast trade winds subside and are interrupted by southerly or *kona* winds. Looking for a silver lining? If it's raining in Waikiki, the wind shift may mean brilliant sunshine on the windward side of the island, which is normally wetter. Head for beautiful Kailua Beach.

Waikiki's hottest months are August and September, although even then, if the temperature hits 90 degrees F (30 degrees C), it makes page one of the newspaper.

Climate The following are average daily maximum and minimum temperatures for Waikiki.

Jan.	76F	24C	May	80F	27C	Sept.	83F	28C
	68	21		70	21		74	23
Feb.	76F	24C	June	81F	27C	Oct.	82F	28C
	68	19		72	22		72	22
Mar.	77F	25C	July	82F	28C	Nov.	80F	27C
	67	19		73	23		70	21
Apr.	78F	26C	Aug.	83F	28C	Dec.	78F	26C
	68	20		74	23		69	21

Current weather information on over 750 cities around the world—450 of them in the United States—is only a phone call away. Call WeatherTrak at 900/370–8725 from a touch-tone phone—at a cost of 75¢ for the first minute, 50¢ each additional minute. The number plays a taped message that tells you to dial a three-digit access code for the destination you're interested in. The code is either the area code (in the United States) or the first three letters of the foreign city. For a list of all access codes, send a stamped, self-addressed envelope to Cities, Box 7000, Dallas, TX 75209. For further information, phone 214/869 –3035 or 800/247–3282.

Festivals and Seasonal Events

Jan.–Mar.: Narcissus Festival. Welcoming in the Chinese New Year are a queen pageant, coronation ball, cooking demonstrations, and a noisy evening of fireworks in Chinatown.
Early Jan.: Queen Emma Museum Open House. To celebrate Queen Emma's birthday, the museum offers free admission. Tel. 808/595–6291.

Early Jan.: Hula Bowl. The annual college all-star football classic is played at Aloha Stadium. Special buses often run from Waikiki. Tel. 808/486–9300.

Late Jan.: NFL Pro Bowl. An all-star football game, involving the National and American conferences of the National Football League, is played annually at Aloha Stadium. Tel. 808/486–9300.

Late Jan.: Robert Burns Night. The clans gather from Canada and mainland United States for a highland fling.

Feb.–Mar.: Cherry Blossom Festival. A celebration of all things Japanese that includes a run, cultural displays, cooking demonstrations, music, and the inevitable queen pageant with a coronation ball. This festival is well done and popular. Tel. 808/522–4153.

Early Feb.: Hawaiian Open Golf Tournament. The top golf pros tee off for $500,000 in prizes at the exclusive Waialae Country Club.

Mid-Feb.: Punahou Carnival. Hawaii's most prestigious school stages an annual fund raiser with rides, arts and crafts, local food, and a great white elephant sale.

Late Feb.: Great Aloha Run. An 8-mile course from Aloha Tower to Aloha Stadium benefits the Variety school.

Early Mar.: "World's Greatest Garage and Plant Sale." Crafts and white elephants go on sale to benefit the American Cancer Society. Blaisdell Exhibition Hall, Ward Ave. and King St., tel. 808/522–0333.

Mid-Mar.: Hawaiian Song Festival and Song Composing Contest. The site is Kapiolani Bandstand, Waikiki, tel. 808/521–9815.

Mid-Mar.: Emerald Ball. The Friendly Sons of St. Patrick celebrate with music and dancing.

Mar. 17: St. Patrick's Day Parade. It goes right down Kalakaua Avenue from Fort DeRussy to Kapiolani Park, and is followed by a boisterous no-host party at a Waikiki hotel.

Late Mar.: Opening Day of the Polo Season. Games are held every Sunday through August, 2 PM, at Dillingham Polo Field, Mokuleia, tel. 808/533–2890.

Mar. 26: Prince Kuhio Day. A state holiday honoring Prince Kuhio. Celebration takes place at the Prince Kuhio Federal Building in downtown Honolulu, and at Sea Life Park (tel. 808/259–7933) and Waimea Falls Park (tel. 808/638–8511).

Apr.: Easter Sunrise Service. The Hawaii Council of Churches holds this popular gathering at Punchbowl National Memorial Cemetery of the Pacific. Special buses run to the crater. Tel. 808/531–4888.

Early Apr.: Bud Light Tin Man Biathlon. Athletes test themselves in a 2.7-mile run and 800-meter swim.

Mid. Apr.: Buddha Day. Flower pageants are staged at temples throughout the Islands.

Mid. Apr.: Carole Kai Bed Race, Parade, and Concert. Big names in town turn out for this zany event centered in Waikiki. It's all for charity. Tel. 808/735–6092.

May 1: Lei Day. The annual flower-filled celebration is held in Kapiolani Park. Winning leis in the annual lei-making contest are on exhibit. There's music, hula, food—and lots of leis for sale, some of them exquisite floral masterpieces. In the evening, there's a concert of Hawaiian music by the famous local group, the Cazimero Brothers, outdoors at the Waikiki Shell.

Early May: Pacific Handcrafters Guild Spring Fair. Some of

Hawaii's best artisans participate. There are demonstrations, food, and entertainment. Ala Moana Park.

Memorial Day: Special military services are held at Punchbowl National Memorial Cemetery of the Pacific. Tel. 808/541–1430.

Late May–early June: Fiftieth State Fair. The Honolulu Jaycees bring together produce exhibits, food booths, entertainment, and amusement rides.

Late May–early June: Festival of the Pacific. A relatively new celebration, this week-long affair of sports, music, songs, and dances has become very popular.

June 11: Kamehameha Day. The Friday before the 11th, the statue of the king who united all the Hawaiian Islands is draped in 25-foot leis. The statue is in downtown Honolulu and makes a great photograph the next morning, when a colorful parade forms at Iolani Palace and proceeds to Ala Moana Park. It's followed by a *ho'olaulea* (street party) in Waikiki.

June–July: Hawaii State Farm Fair. Held on the grounds of Honolulu's McKinley High School, it features farm products, food booths, and amusement rides.

Mid-July: Mid-Summer's Night Gleam. Foster Botanic Garden in downtown Honolulu opens at night for a moonlight walk and entertainment. Tel. 808/537–1708.

Mid-July: Prince Lot Hula Festival. A whole day of ancient and modern hula unfolds beneath the towering trees of Oahu's Moanalua Gardens. Tel. 808/839–5334.

Late July: Annual Ukulele Festival. Hundreds of ukulele players perform at Kapiolani Bandstand in Waikiki.

End of July–Aug. Bon Odori Season. Buddhist temples throughout the Islands invite all to the festivals honoring ancestors. A highlight is the Japanese bon dancing. In mid-July, the Haleiwa Jodo Mission on Oahu's North Shore has a beautiful floating lantern ceremony. Tel. 808/637–4382.

Early Aug.: Makahiki. Hawaiian sports and games, a farm fair, and traditional crafts are featured in this ancient annual celebration. Kapiolani Park, Waikiki.

Early Aug.: Hula Festival. Participants of Honolulu's Summer Fun children's classes plus hula schools (both adults and children) perform at Waikiki's Kapiolani Bandstand on three successive Sundays. Tel. 808/521–9815.

Aug. 19: Admission Day. A state holiday recognizes Hawaii's admission to statehood.

Early Sept.: Waikiki Rough Water Swim. All ages and categories compete in a 2-mile swim to benefit the American Lung Association. Tel. 808/537–5966.

Late Sept.: Aloha Week Festival. Major events include Hawaiian pageantry, canoe races, street parties, entertainment, and a grand parade through Waikiki.

Late Sept.: A Day at Queen Emma Summer Palace. The Daughters of Hawaii stage a day of Hawaiian arts, crafts, and entertainment at the Queen Emma Summer Palace, Honolulu. Tel. 808/ 595–6291.

Early Oct.: Waimea Falls Park Makahiki. The ancient makahiki was a harvest festival. The tradition is carried out at Waimea Falls Park, Oahu, with a day of games, music, hula competition, and food. Tel. 808/638–8511.

Early Oct.: Pacific Handcrafters Guild Fair. A weekend of craft demonstrations, ethnic foods, and entertainment at Ala Moana Park, Honolulu.

Mid-Oct.: Bankoh Molokai Hoe. The annual Molokai to Oahu canoe race finishes at Fort DeRussy Beach, Waikiki.

Late Aug.: Best Little Chili Cookoff. Honolulu Community Theatre is the beneficiary of this entertaining tasting held at Restaurant Row, near downtown Honolulu. Tel. 808/523–1307.

Mid-Oct.: Orchid Show. It's a beauty at the Blaisdell Center, Honolulu. Tel. 808/527–5400.

End of Nov.: Mission Houses Museum Annual Christmas Fair. Artists and craftspeople present their wares in an open market at the historic houses of Hawaii's first Yankee missionaries in downtown Honolulu. Tel. 808/531–0481.

Late Nov.–early Dec.: Hawaii International Film Festival. A visual feast of award-winning cinematography from the United States, Asia, and the Pacific illustrates the theme "When Strangers Meet." Several theaters in Waikiki participate. Tel. 808/944–7200.

Dec.: Triple Crown of Surfing. Times, dates, and beaches are based on wave conditions as the top pro surfers gather for the winter waves on Oahu's North Shore. All month.

Early Dec.: Pacific Handcrafters Guild Christmas Fair. Here's a chance to buy some inexpensive art for gifts. Thomas Square, Honolulu.

Early Dec.: Honolulu Marathon. Watch or run in one of the country's most popular marathons.

Early Dec.: Bodhi Day. The Buddhist community celebrates the Day of Enlightenment.

Dec. 25: Christmas. The hotels outdo each other in extravagant exhibits. When local children are small, part of their holiday treat is going from lobby to lobby to see the fantastic displays —towering poinsettia trees (Kahala Hilton, Ilikai), Santa arriving by outrigger (Kahala Hilton), and a gingerbread town (Hyatt Regency), to name a few of the most memorable. There are concerts by children's choirs and special treats for guest children. Christmas won't be white, but it will be very merry.

Christmas Day: Aloha Bowl. The popular game is a collegiate event at Aloha Stadium, Oahu. Tel. 808/488–9509.

What to Pack

You can pack lightly because Hawaii is casual. Bare feet, bathing suits, and comfortable, informal clothing are the norm.

The Man's Suitcase In the Hawaiian Islands, there's a saying that when a man wears a suit during the day, he's either going for a loan or he's a lawyer trying a case. Only a few upscale Waikiki restaurants require a jacket for dinner, and none requires a tie. Hawaii regulars wear their jackets on the plane—just in case—and many don't put them on again until the return flight. The aloha shirt is accepted dress in Hawaii for business and most social occasions. A visitor can easily buy one after arriving in Waikiki (*see* Chapter 5).

Shorts are acceptable daytime attire, along with a T-shirt or polo shirt. If you want to be marked as a tourist, wear your shorts with dark shoes and white socks. Local-style casual footwear consists of tennis or running shoes, sandals, or rubber slippers. You'll also see a lot of bare feet, but state law requires that footwear be worn in all food establishments.

Pack your toiletries, underwear, and a pair or two of easy-care slacks to wear with those aloha shirts, and you're all set.

Female Fashion During the winter months, be sure to bring a sweater or wrap for the evening because the trade winds cool things off as soon as the sun goes down. If you have an elaborate coiffure, a scarf will help keep it from getting windblown.

Sundresses, shorts, and tops are fine for daytime. During the summer months, synthetic slacks and shirts, although easy to care for, can get uncomfortably warm. If you have a long slip, bring it for the muumuu you say you won't buy, but probably will. As for shoes, sandals and tennis or running shoes are fine for daytime, and sandals are perfect for the evening. If you wear boots, you'll wish you hadn't.

If you don't own a pareu, buy one in Hawaii. It's simply a length (about 1½ yards long) of light cotton in a tropical motif that can be worn as a beachwrap, a skirt, or a dozen other wrap-up fashions. A pareu is useful wherever you go, regardless of climate. It makes a good bathrobe, so you don't have to pack one. You can even tie it up as a handbag or sit on it at the beach.

For Everyone Don't forget your bathing suit. Sooner or later, the crystal clear water tempts even the most sedentary landlubber. Of course, bathing suits are easy to find in Hawaii. Shops are crammed with the latest styles. If you wear a bathing cap, bring one; you can waste hours searching for one.

Probably the most important thing to tuck in your suitcase is sunscreen. This is the tropics, and the ultraviolet rays are much more powerful than those to which you are accustomed. Doctors advise putting on sunscreen when you get up in the morning. Women can wear it as a moisturizer under makeup. The upper chest area of a woman is hypopigmented and should be protected. Don't forget to reapply sunscreen periodically during the day, since perspiration can wash it away. Consider using sunscreens with a sun protection factor (SPF) of 15 or higher. There are many tanning oils on the market in Hawaii, including coconut and kukui oils, but doctors warn that they merely sauté your skin. Too many Hawaiian vacations have been spoiled by sunburn.

Visitors who wear glasses are wise to pack an extra pair. Eyeglasses are easy to lose, and you can waste days of your precious Hawaiian holiday replacing them.

If you don't bring your camera and plenty of film, you'll wish you did. Much of Hawaii is so beautiful that all you have to do is point and shoot to get great photographs. Overnight processing is available at many locations in Waikiki.

It's a good idea to tuck in a few jumbo zip-lock plastic bags when you travel—they're ideal for wet swimsuits or food souvenirs that might leak. All hotels in Hawaii provide beach towels. Some hotels provide hair dryers and some don't. Unless you know for sure, bring your own. If you forget something, you can probably find it at your hotel sundry store or at one of the 24 ABC drugstores in and around Waikiki.

Cash Machines

Virtually all U.S. banks belong to a network of ATMs (Automatic Teller Machines), which gobble up bank cards and spit out cash 24 hours a day in cities throughout the country. There are some eight major networks in the United States, the largest of which are Cirrus, owned by MasterCard, and Plus, affiliated with Visa. Some banks belong to more than one network. These cards are not automatically issued; you have to ask for them. If your bank doesn't belong to at least one network, you should consider moving your account, for ATMs are becoming as essential as check cashing. Cards issued by Visa and MasterCard may also be used in the ATMs, but the fees are usually higher than the fees on bank cards, and there is a daily interest charge on the "loan," even if monthly bills are paid on time. Each network has a toll-free number you can call to locate machines in a given city. The Cirrus number is 800/4–CIRRUS; the Plus number is 800/THE–PLUS. Check with your bank for fees and for the amount of cash you can withdraw on any given day.

Waikiki has cash machines at **Bank of Hawaii** (2220 Kalakaua Ave.), **Central Pacific Bank** (Hyatt Regency Hotel, 2424 Kalakaua Ave.), **City Bank** (2301 Kuhio St.), **First Hawaiian Bank** (2181 Kalakaua Ave.), **First Nationwide Bank** (334 Seaside Ave.), **Hawaii National Bank** (321 Seaside Ave.), and **Liberty Bank** (Royal Hawaiian Shopping Center). Before you leave home, ask your local bank for a list of banks in Hawaii that will honor your bank cash card.

Insurance

Travelers may seek insurance coverage in three areas: health and accident, loss of luggage, and trip cancellation. Your first step is to review your existing health and homeowner policies; some health insurance plans cover health expenses incurred while traveling, some major medical plans cover emergency transportation, and some homeowner policies cover the theft of luggage.

Health and Accident Several companies offer coverage designed to supplement existing health insurance for travelers:

Carefree Travel Insurance (Box 310, 120 Mineola Blvd., Mineola, NY 11501, tel. 516/294–0220 or 800/645–2424) provides coverage for medical evacuation. It also offers 24-hour medical phone advice.

Health Care Abroad, International Underwriters Group (243 Church St., Vienna, VA 22180, tel. 703/281–9500 or 800/237–6615), offers comprehensive medical coverage, including emergency evacuation, for trips of 10–90 days.

International SOS Insurance (Box 11568, Philadelphia, PA 19116, tel. 215/244–1500 or 800/523–8930) does not offer medical insurance but provides medical evacuation services to its clients, who are often international corporations.

Travel Guard International, underwritten by Cygna (1100 Centerpoint Dr., Stevens Point, WI 54481, tel. 715/345–0505 or 800/782–5151) offers medical insurance, with coverage for emergency evacuation when Travel Guard's representatives in the United States say it is necessary.

For British Travelers We recommend that to cover health and motoring mishaps, you insure yourself with **Europ Assistance** (252 High St., Croydon, Surrey CRO INF, tel. 081/680–1234).

Lost Luggage The loss of luggage is usually covered as part of a comprehensive travel insurance package that includes personal accident, trip cancellation, and sometimes default and bankruptcy insurance. Several companies offer comprehensive policies:

Access America Inc., a subsidiary of Blue Cross-Blue Shield (Box 807, New York, NY 10163, tel. 800/851–2800).

Near Services, (450 Prairie Ave., Suite 101, Calumet City, IL 60409, tel. 708/868–6700 or 800/654–6700).

Travel Guard International (*see* Health and Accident Insurance above).

For British Travelers It is also wise to take out insurance to cover the loss of luggage (although check that such loss isn't already covered in any existing homeowner's policies you may have). Trip-cancellation insurance is another wise buy. **The Association of British Insurers** (Aldermary House, Queen St., London EC4N 1TT, tel. 071/248–4477) will give comprehensive advice on all aspects of vacation insurance.

Trip Cancellation Flight insurance is often included in the price of a ticket when paid for with American Express, Visa, and other major credit and charge cards. It is usually included in combination travel insurance packages available from most tour operators, travel agents, and insurance agents.

Traveling with Film

If your camera is new, shoot and develop a few rolls of film before leaving home. Pack some lens tissue and an extra battery for your built-in light meter. Invest about $10 in a skylight filter and screw it onto the front of your lens. It will protect the lens and reduce haze.

Film doesn't survive hot weather. If you're driving in summer, don't store film in the glove compartment or on the shelf under the rear window. Put it behind the front seat on the floor, on the side opposite the exhaust pipe.

On a plane trip, never pack unprocessed film in check-in luggage; if your bags get X-rayed, say goodbye to your pictures. Always carry undeveloped film with you through airport security and ask to have it inspected by hand. (It helps to isolate your film in a plastic bag, ready for quick inspection.) Inspectors at American airports are required by law to honor requests for hand inspection.

The newer airport scanning machines—used in all U.S. airports—are safe for anything from five to 500 scans, depending on the speed of your film. The effects are cumulative; you can put the same roll of film through several scans without worry. After five scans, though, you're asking for trouble.

If your film gets fogged and you want an explanation, send it to the National Association of Photographic Manufacturers (550 Mamaroneck Ave., Harrison, NY 10528), which will try to determine what went wrong. The service is free.

Traveling with Children

Publications *Family Travel Times*, an 8- to 12-page newsletter, is published 10 times a year by TWYCH (Travel with Your Children, 80 Eighth Ave., New York, NY 10011, tel. 212/206–0688). Subscription includes access to back issues and twice-weekly opportunities to call in for specific advice. *Great Vacations with Your Kids: The Complete Guide to Family Vacations in the U.S.* by Dorothy Ann Jordon and Marjorie Adoff Cohen (E. P. Dutton, New York) details everything from city vacations to adventure vacations to child-care resources.

Condo Rentals See *The Condo Lux Vacationer's Guide to Condominium Rentals in the Southwest and Hawaii* by Jill Little (Vintage Books/Random House, New York).

Home Exchange See *Home Exchanging: A Complete Sourcebook for Travelers at Home or Abroad* by James Dearing (Globe Pequot Press, Box Q, Chester, CT 06412, tel. 800/243–0495; in CT, tel. 800/962–0973).

Getting There On domestic flights, children under 2 who are not occupying a seat travel free. Various discounts apply to children ages 2–12. Regulations about infant travel on airplanes are in the process of changing. Until they do, however, if you want to be sure your infant is secured in his/her own safety seat, you must buy a separate ticket and bring your own infant car seat. (Check with the airline in advance; certain seats aren't allowed. Or write for the booklet *Child/Infant Safety Seats Acceptable for Use in Aircraft*, from the Federal Aviation Administration, APA-200, 800 Independence Ave. SW, Washington, DC 20591, tel. 202/267–3479.) Some airlines allow babies to travel in their own safety seats at no charge if there's a spare seat on the plane available, otherwise safety seats will be stored and the child will have to be held by a parent. If you opt to hold your baby on your lap, do so with the infant outside the seat belt so he or she won't be crushed in case of a sudden stop.

Also inquire about special children's meals or snacks. See the February 1990 and 1992 issues of *Family Travel Times* for "TWYCH's Airline Guide," which contains a rundown of the children's services offered by 46 airlines.

In the Waikiki Area Some hotels in and around Waikiki offer special programs for children, which are supervised by adults. These programs may include such activities as arts and crafts, sports, and treasure hunts. Among the hotels offering programs for children are the Hilton Hawaiian Village, the Kahala Hilton, and the Sheraton Waikiki (*see* Chapter 8 for addresses and numbers). About 2,500 children annually participate in Sheraton's "Keiki Aloha Program," headquartered at the Sheraton Waikiki and offered free to guests of all Sheraton hotels in Waikiki. The imaginative program includes evening activities so parents may dine and dance on their own. You may wish to find out beforehand if the hotel you are planning to stay at has special programs for children.

Car Rental Hawaii state law requires that infants be restrained in car seats. Check to be sure your rental company has a seat available for you.

Hints for Disabled Travelers

The Information Center for Individuals with Disabilities (Fort Point Pl., 1st floor, 27 Wormwood St., Boston, MA 02110, tel. 617/727–5540) offers useful problem-solving assistance, including lists of travel agents who specialize in tours for the disabled.
Moss Rehabilitation Hospital Travel Information Service (12th St. and Taber Rd., Philadelphia, PA 19141, tel. 215/329–5715) provides information on tourist sights, transportation, and accommodations in destinations around the world. The fee is $5 for each destination. Allow one month for delivery.
Mobility International (Box 3551, Eugene, OR 97403, tel. 503/

343–1284) has information on accommodations, organized study, and so forth around the world.

The Society for the Advancement of Travel for the Handicapped (26 Court St., Brooklyn, NY 11242, tel. 718/858–5483) offers access information. The annual membership is $40 or $25 for senior travelers and students. Send a stamped, self-addressed envelope.

The Itinerary (Box 1084, Bayonne, NJ 07002, tel. 201/858–3400) is a bimonthly travel magazine for the disabled.

Greyhound (tel. 800/531–5332) will carry a disabled person and a companion for the price of a single fare. **Amtrak** (tel. 800/USA–RAIL) requests 24-hour notice to provide redcap service, special seats, and a 25% discount.

In the Waikiki Area Many of Hawaii's major attractions, shopping centers, and restaurants have wheelchair ramps, and the better hotels offer entry and exit ramps, grab bars, low telephones, and parking stalls. **The Commission on Persons with Disabilities** (5 Waterfront Plaza, Suite 210, 500 Ala Moana Blvd., Honolulu 96813, tel. 808/548–7606) offers a free *Traveler's Guide*, with information to help the disabled plan a visit to Hawaii. Included are listings of facilities and their accessibility features and a mobility map of Waikiki.

You can pick up a handicapped-parking pass at the **Department of Transportation Services** (650 S. King St., Honolulu 96813, tel. 808/523–4021). If you already have a windshield card from your own state, that's all you need. Curb-to-curb service is offered through **Handi-Vans** (tel. 808/524–4626) if it is arranged on a 24-hour notice. You must meet the Handi-vans administrator once in person, however, to prove your disability. All rides cost $1. **Handi-Cabs of the Pacific** (tel. 808/524–3866) is a private taxi company with van ramps. It operates on Oahu for an $8 curbside pickup charge plus $1.95 per mile, and offers free wheelchairs to transfer passengers. **Avis** (tel. 800/831–8000) rents hand controls for cars. Wheelchairs, walkers, oxygen, lifts, and overbed tables can be rented from **AA Medical Equipment** (711 S. Queen St., Honolulu 96813, tel. 808/537–5933) and **Abbey Medical** (500 Ala Kawa St., Honolulu, 96817, tel. 808/845–5000). You must contact these companies in advance.

Hints for Older Travelers

The American Association of Retired Persons (AARP, 1909 K St. NW, Washington, DC 20049, tel. 202/662–4850) has two programs for independent travelers: (1) The Purchase Privilege Program, which offers discounts on hotels, airfare, car rentals, and sightseeing, and (2) the AARP Motoring Plan, which offers emergency aid and trip-routing information for an annual fee of $29.95 per couple. The AARP also arranges group tours through **Olson-Travelworld** (100 N. Sepulveda Blvd., El Segundo, CA 90245, tel. 213/615–0711 or 800/421–2255). As of January 1991, tours will be arranged by **American Express Vacations** (*see* Tour Groups, above). AARP members must be age 50 or older. Annual dues are $5 per person or per couple.

When using an AARP or other identification card, ask for a reduced hotel rate at the time you make your reservation, not when you check out. At restaurants, show your card to the maître d' before you're seated, since discounts may be limited to certain set menus, days, or hours. When renting a car, remember that economy cars, priced at promotional rates, may cost less than cars that are available with your ID card.

Elderhostel (80 Boylston St., Suite 400, Boston, MA 02116, tel. 617/426–7788) is an innovative 13-year-old program for people aged 60 and older. Participants live in dormitories on some 1,200 campuses around the world. Mornings are devoted to lectures and seminars; afternoons, to sightseeing and field trips. The all-inclusive fee for 2–3 week trips, including room, board, tuition, and round-trip transportation, is $1,700–$3,200.

Golden Age Passport is a free lifetime pass to all parks, monuments, and recreation areas run by the federal government. People over age 62 may pick it up in person at any national park that charges admission. A driver's license or other proof of age is required.

Mature Outlook (6001 N. Clark St., Chicago, IL 60660, tel. 800/336–6330), a subsidiary of Sears Roebuck & Co., is a travel club for people over age 50, with hotel and motel discounts and a bi-monthly newsletter. Annual membership is $9.95 per couple. Instant membership is available at participating Holiday Inns.

National Council of Senior Citizens (925 15th St. NW, Washington, DC 20005, tel. 202/347–8800) is a nonprofit advocacy group with some 5,000 local clubs across the country. Annual membership is $12 per person or per couple. Members receive a monthly newspaper with travel information and an ID card for reduced-rate hotels and car rentals.

Travel Industry and Disabled Exchange (TIDE, 5435 Donna Ave., Tarzana, CA 91356, tel. 818/343–6339) is an industry-based organization with a $15 per person annual membership fee. Members receive a quarterly newsletter and information on travel agencies and tours.

Hawaiian Language

The Hawaiian language is unlike anything normally heard by the average traveler. But given the chance, say at a traditional church service or a local ceremony, visitors will find the soft, rolling language of the Islands both interesting and refreshing to the ear.

Although an understanding of Hawaiian is by no means required, *malihinis*, or newcomers, will find plenty of opportunities to pick up a few of the local words and phrases. In fact, traditional names and expressions are still in such wide usage today that visitors will be hard pressed not to read or hear them each day of their visit. Such exposure adds nothing but enrichment to any stay. With a basic understanding and some uninhibited practice, anyone can have enough command of the local tongue to ask for directions by street names and to order off the neighborhood restaurant menus.

Simplifying the learning process is the fact that the Hawaiian language contains only seven consonants—H,K,L,M,N,P, and W—and the five vowels. All syllables and all words end in a vowel. Each vowel, with the exception of diphthongized double vowels such as *au* (pronounced ow) or *ai* (pronounced eye), is pronounced separately. *Aa*, the word for rough lava, for example, is pronounced ah-ah.

Although some Hawaiian words have only vowels, most also contain some combination consonants as well. Consonants are never doubled, and they always begin syllables, as in Ka-me-ha-me-ha.

The accent in most Hawaiian words falls on the penultimate syllable. Since most Hawaiian words are two syllables, the accent falls on the first syllable as in KO-na, PA-li, and KA-na. The exception occurs when the vowels in the second syllable become diphthongized, as in ha-PAI and ma-KAI, which are fundamentally ha-PA-i and ma-KA-i.

Pronunciation is simple. Use the following table as a guide to pronounce

A "uh" as in above
E "ay" as in weigh
I "ee" as in marine
O "oh" as in no
U "oo" as in true

Consonants mirror their English equivalents, with the exception of W. When the letter begins the last syllable of a word, it is sometimes pronounced as a V. Awa, the Polynesian drink, is pronounced "ava"; Ewa plantation is pronounced "Eva."

What follows is a glossary of some of the most commonly used Hawaiian words. Don't be afraid to give them a try. Hawaii residents appreciate visitors who at least try to pick up the local language—no matter how fractured the pronunciation.

aa—rough, crumbling lava, contrasting with *pahoehoe*, which is smooth.
ae—yes.
akamai—smart, clever, possessing savoir-faire.
ala—a road, path, or trail.
alii—a Hawaiian chief, a member of the chiefly class; also plural.
aloha—love, affection, kindness. Also a salutation meaning both greetings and farewell.
aole—no.
auwai—a ditch.
auwe—alas, woe is me!
ehu—a red-haired Hawaiian.
ewa—in the direction of Ewa plantation, west of Honolulu.
hala—the pandanus tree, whose leaves *(lauhala)* are used to make baskets and plaited mats.
hale—a house.
hana—to work.
haole—originally a stranger or foreigner. Since the first foreigners were Caucasian, *haole* now means a Caucasian person.
hapa—a part, sometimes a half.
hapa haole—part *haole*, a person of mixed racial background, part of which is Caucasian.
hauoli—to rejoice. *Hauoli Makahiki Hou* means Happy New Year.
heiau—an ancient Hawaiian place of worship.
holo—to run.
holoholo—to go for a walk, ride, or sail.
holoku—a long Hawaiian dress, somewhat fitted, with a scoop neck and a train. Influenced by European fashion, it was worn at court.
holomuu—a recent cross between a *holoku* and a *muumuu*,

less fitted than the former but less voluminous than the latter, and having no train.

honi—to kiss, a kiss. A phrase that some tourists may find useful, quoted from a popular *hula*, is *Honi Kaua wikiwiki:* Kiss me quick!

hoomalimali—flattery, a deceptive "line," bunk, baloney, hooey.

huhu—angry.

hui—a group, club, or assembly. There are church *huis* and social *huis*.

hukilau—a seine, a communal fishing party in which everyone helps to drive the fish into a huge net, pull it in, and divide the catch.

hula—the dance of Hawaii.

ipo—sweetheart.

ka—the definite article.

kahuna—a priest, doctor, or other trained person of old Hawaii, endowed with special professional skills that often included the gift of prophecy or other supernatural powers.

kai—the sea, salt water.

kalo—the taro plant from whose root *poi* is made.

kamaaina—literally, a child of the soil, it refers to people who were born in the Islands or have lived there for a long time.

kanaka—originally a man or humanity in general, it is now used to denote a male Hawaiian or part-Hawaiian.

kane—a man, a husband. If you see this word on a door, it's the men's room.

kapa—also called *tapa*, a cloth made of beaten bark and usually dyed and stamped with a primitive geometric design.

kapakahi—crooked, cockeyed, uneven. You've got your hat on *kapakahi*.

kapu—keep out, prohibited. This is the Hawaiian version of the more widely known Tongan word *tabu* (taboo).

keiki—a child; *keikikane* is a boy child, *keikiwahine* a girl.

kokua—help.

kona—the south, also the south or leeward side of the islands from which the *kona* wind and *kona* rain come.

kuleana—a homestead or small plot of ground on which a family has been installed for some generations without necessarily owning it. By extension, *kuleana* is used to denote any area or department in which one has a special interest or prerogative. You'll hear it used this way: If you want to hire a surfboard, see Moki; that's his *kuleana*. And conversely, I can't help you with that; that's not my *kuleana*.

lamalama—to fish with a torch.

lanai—a porch, a covered pavilion, an outdoor living room. Almost every house in Hawaii has one.

lani—heaven, the sky.

lauhala—the leaf of the *hala* or pandanus tree, widely used in Hawaiian handcrafts.

lei—a garland of flowers.

luna—a plantation overseer or foreman.

mahalo—thank you.

makai—toward the sea.

malihini—a newcomer to the Islands.

mana—the spiritual power that the Hawaiians believed to inhabit all things and creatures.

manawahi—free, gratis.

mauka—toward the mountains.

mauna—mountain.

mele—a Hawaiian song or chant, often of epic proportions.
menehune—a Hawaiian pixie. The *menehunes* were a legendary race of little people who accomplished prodigious work, like building fishponds and temples in the course of a single night.
moana—the ocean.
muumuu—the voluminous dress in which the missionaries enveloped Hawaiian women. Now made up in bright printed cottons and silks, it is an indispensable garment in a Hawaiian woman's wardrobe.
nani—beautiful.
nui—big.
pake—a Chinese. Give this *pake* boy some rice.
palapala—book, printing.
pali—a cliff, precipice.
panini—cactus.
paniolo—a Hawaiian cowboy.
pau—finished, done.
pilikia—trouble. The Hawaiian word is much more widely used here than its English equivalent.
puka—a hole.
pupule—crazy, like the celebrated Princess Pupule. This word has replaced its English equivalent in local usage.
wahine—a female, a woman, a wife, and a sign on the ladies' room door.
wai—fresh water, as opposed to salt water, which is *kai*.
wikiwiki—to hurry, hurry up.

Pidgin English is the unofficial language of Hawaii. It is heard everywhere: on ranches, in warehouses, on beaches, and in the hallowed halls (though not in the classrooms) of the University of Hawaii. It's still English and not much tougher to follow than Brooklynese; it just takes a little getting used to.

Further Reading

For a good historical and adventure novel set on the Hawaiian Islands, start with *Hawaii*, by James A. Michener. Other works of fiction set in the Hawaiian Islands include Margaret M. Dukore's *Bloom*, a romance set in Honolulu; *Death March* by Ralph Glendinning, a suspense novel; *Waimea Summer* by John Dominis Holt, an autobiographical novel about a boy's experiences in Hawaii; James Jones's novel *From Here to Eternity*, about army life in pre-Pearl Harbor days; Jack London's *Stories of Hawaii;* Kathleen Mellen's *In a Hawaiian Valley*, stories of Hawaiian home life (currently out of print, but worth looking for in a library); and N. Richard Nash's *East Wind, Rain*, a novel of love and espionage at Pearl Harbor, 1941.

Garrett Hongo often writes about Hawaii in his two poetry collections, *Yellow Light* and *The River of Heaven*. Two anthologies of Hawaii-related literature include *A Hawaiian Reader* and *The Spell of Hawaii*, both edited by A. Grove Day and Carl Stroven.

Hawaii's history may be explored in Gwenfread Allen's *Hawaii's War Years, 1941–1945;* Paul Bailey's *Those Kings and Queens of Old Hawaii; Shoal of Time*, Gavan Davis's history of the Hawaiian Islands; and Edward Joesting's *Hawaii: An Uncommon History*. Two other nonfiction books worth investigating are Robert Louis Stevenson's *Travels in Hawaii* and Mark Twain's *Letters from Hawaii*.

Now in its 13th year of publication, *ALOHA, The Magazine of Hawaii and the Pacific* (49 S. Hotel St., Suite 309, Honolulu, HI 96813, 808/523-9871), is a valuable source of information about the Fiftieth State and other Pacific destinations; it covers a wide range of topics including history, the arts, business, people, sports, food, interiors, music and dance, flora and fauna, Pacific-related books, and real estate. *ALOHA* is a bimonthly publication; subscription rates are $14.95 a year (six issues). The new publication on the block (four years old) is *Pleasant HAWAII, The Aloha State Magazine* (270 Lewers St., Penthouse, Honolulu, HI 96815, tel. 808/924-7299). Packed with magnificent photography, timely information, and stories by prize-winning writers, it is both a handy planning tool and a beautiful "keeper." *Pleasant HAWAII* is a bimonthly publication; subscription rates are $14.50 a year (six issues).

Arriving and Departing

By Plane

From the Mainland United States Honolulu International Airport is one of the busiest in the nation. It has been completely renovated and is only 20 minutes from Waikiki. Flying time from the West Coast is 4½ hours.

American carriers serving Hawaii include **United, Northwest, American, Continental, Delta, TWA, Hawaiian, Pan Am, Air America, Trans Continental Airlines,** and **America West.** At press time, **U.S. Air** had announced plans to begin Hawaii service. Most flights to Hawaii originate in Los Angeles or San Francisco, which, of course, means they are nonstop. There are also nonstop flights from Dallas/Fort Worth, Chicago, Seattle, and San Diego. There are direct flights (which means there are one or more stops along the route, but you don't have to change planes) from Anchorage, New York, and other cities in the East, Southwest, and Midwest. Connecting flights are available from almost every American city.

By law, foreign carriers serving Hawaii may not carry passengers from other American cities. Bringing passengers from foreign destinations are **Qantas, Canadian Pacific Air, Air Canada, Japan Air Lines, Philippine Air Lines, Air New Zealand, China Air Lines, Korean Air Lines, Singapore Airlines, Air Tungaru, Air Niugini, All Nippon Airways, UTA French Airlines, Air Micronesia, Canadian Airlines International, Garuda Indonesia, Malaysian Airlines,** and **Wardair Canada.**

From the United Kingdom **American, Continental, Delta,** and **TWA** are among the airlines that fly to Honolulu. An APEX ticket costs about £559 for a midweek flight, plus taxes. Ring around for the best offers.

Trailfinders (42–48 Earl's Court Rd., Kensington, London W8 6EJ, tel. 071/938–3366) can arrange flights to Honolulu from £535.

Discount Flights Charter flights are the least expensive and the least reliable— with chronically late departures and occasional cancellations. They also tend to depart less frequently (usually once a week) than do regularly scheduled flights. If the savings are worth the potential annoyance, charter flights serving Honolulu International Airport include **Air America** (808/834–7172 or 800/323–8052) and **Trans Air** (808/833–5557). Consult your local travel agent for further information.

Smoking Smoking is banned on all routes within the 48 contiguous states; within the states of Hawaii and Alaska; to and from the U.S. Virgin Islands and Puerto Rico; and on flights of under six hours to and from Hawaii and Alaska. The rule applies to both domestic and foreign carriers.

On a flight where smoking is permitted, you can request a nonsmoking seat during check-in or when you book your ticket. If the airline tells you there are no seats available in the nonsmoking section, insist on one: Department of Transportation regulations require carriers to find seats for all nonsmokers, provided they meet check-in time restrictions. These regulations apply to all international flights on domestic carriers; however, the Department of Transportation does not have jurisdiction over foreign carriers traveling out of, or into the US.

Carry-on Luggage New rules have been in effect since January 1, 1988, on United States airlines regarding carry-on luggage. The model for these new rules was agreed to by the airlines in December 1987 and then circulated by the Air Transport Association with the understanding that each airline would present its own version.

Under the model, passengers are limited to two carry-on bags. For a bag you wish to store under the seat, the maximum dimensions are 9″ x 14″ x 22″, a total of 45″. For bags that can be hung in a closet or on a luggage rack, the maximum dimensions are 4″ x 23″ x 45″, a total of 72″. For bags you wish to store in an overhead bin, the maximum dimensions are 10″ x 14″ x 36″, a total of 60″. Your two carryons must each fit one of these sets of dimensions, and any item that exceeds the specified dimensions will generally be rejected as a carryon and handled as checked baggage. Keep in mind that an airline can adapt these rules to circumstances, so on an especially crowded flight, don't be surprised if you are allowed only one carry-on bag.

In addition to the two carryons, the rules list eight items that may also be brought aboard: a handbag (pocketbook or purse), an overcoat or wrap, an umbrella, a camera, a reasonable amount of reading material, an infant bag, crutches, a cane, braces, or other prosthetic devices. An infant/child safety seat can also be brought aboard if parents have purchased a ticket for the child or if there is space in the cabin.

Note that these regulations are for U.S. airlines only. Foreign airlines generally allow one piece of carry-on luggage in tourist class in addition to handbags and bags filled with duty-free goods. Passengers in first and business class are also allowed to carry on one garment bag. It is best to check with the airline ahead of time to find out its exact rules regarding carry-on luggage.

Checked Luggage U.S. airlines allow passengers to check in two suitcases whose total dimensions (length plus width plus height) do not exceed 60″, and whose weight does not exceed 70 pounds.

Rules governing foreign airlines vary from airline to airline, so check with your travel agent or the airline itself before you go. All the airlines allow passengers to check in two bags. In general, expect the weight restriction on the two bags to be not more than 70 lbs. each, and the size restrictions on the bags to be 62″ total dimensions.

Luggage Insurance Airlines are responsible for lost or damaged property only up to $1,250 per passenger on domestic flights, $9.07 per pound (or $20 per kilo) for checked baggage on international flights, and up to $400 per passenger for unchecked baggage on international flights. If you're carrying valuables, either take them with you on the airplane or purchase extra insurance for lost luggage. Some airlines will issue additional luggage insurance when you check in, but many do not. One that does is **American Airlines.** Its additional insurance is only for domestic flights or flights to Canada. The rate is $1 for every $100 valuation, with a maximum of $400 valuation per passenger; hand luggage is not included.

Insurance for lost, damaged, or stolen luggage is available through travel agents or directly through various insurance companies. Two that issue luggage insurance are **Tele-Trip** (tel. 800/228–9792), a subsidiary of Mutual of Omaha, and **The Travelers Insurance Co.** Tele-Trip operates sales booths at airports and issues insurance through travel agents. Tele-Trip will insure checked luggage for up to 180 days and for $500–$3,000 valuation. For 1–3 days, the rate for a $500 valuation is $8.25; for 180 days, $100. The Travelers Insurance Co. will insure checked or hand luggage for $500–$2,000 valuation per person, also for a maximum of 180 days. The rate for 1–5 days for $500 valuation is $10; for 180 days, $85. For more information, write: The Travelers Insurance Co., Ticket and Travel Dept., 1 Tower Sq., Hartford, CT 06183. Both companies offer the same rates on domestic and international flights. Check the travel pages of your Sunday newspaper for the names of other companies that insure luggage. Before you go, itemize the contents of each bag in case you need to file an insurance claim. Be certain to put your home address on each piece of luggage, including carry-on bags. If your luggage is stolen and later recovered, the airline must deliver the luggage to your home free of charge.

Between the Airport and Waikiki There are taxis right at the airport exit. At $1.40 start-up plus 20¢ for each ½ mile, the fare will run approximately $13 plus a tip. Drivers are also allowed to charge 30¢ per suitcase. **Terminal Transportation** runs an airport shuttle service to Waikiki (tel. 808/836–0317. Cost: $5). The municipal bus is only 50¢, but you are allowed only one bag which must fit on your lap. Some hotels have their own pickup service. Check when you book your reservations.

If you have extra time at the airport, you will be able to visit the new **Pacific Aerospace Museum** (tel. 808/531–7747) on the upper level of the central concourse of the main terminal. At press time it was still not opened, and a report was unavailable.

Lei Greeting Many visitors are disappointed to find that everyone arriving in Hawaii is not automatically given a lei. With the visitor count at almost 6 million, doing so would bankrupt the state. If you have booked through a tour company and are being met at the airport, you will probably be given a lei by the person who meets you. If you have friends meeting you, most definitely they will have a lei for you. If you are traveling independently, you can arrange for a lei greeting from **Greeters of Hawaii** (Box 29638, Honolulu 96820, tel. 808/836–0161); it requires 48 hours notice. Cost: $9.95 to $33.95 per person, add $10 for late notification.

The standard $9.95 lei usually contains orchids or an orchid-carnation mixture. Being draped in flowers is definitely one of the pleasures of arriving in the Islands. Surprise your traveling companion.

By Ship

Boat Day used to be the biggest day of the week. Jet travel has almost obscured that custom, and it's too bad, because arriving in Hawaii by ship is a great experience. If you have the time, it is one sure way to unwind. Many cruises are planned a year or more in advance and fill up fast. Because of customs regulations, if you sail on a foreign ship from any U.S. port, you must return with that ship to that port. If you arrive in Hawaii from a foreign port, you may disembark in Honolulu. Most cruise-ship companies today offer a fare that includes round-trip air travel to the point of embarkation.

Cunard/N.A.C. Line, Royal Cruises, P & O/Princess Cruises and **Royal Viking** have cruise ships passing through Honolulu once or twice a year.

Car Rentals

The cost of shipping a car by freighter is at least $500. We advise leaving your car at home and renting one.

There's absolutely no need to rent a car if you don't plan to leave Waikiki. In fact, it will be a nuisance with all the one-way streets and the difficulty in parking. If you plan to do some sightseeing outside Waikiki, a number of highly competitive rental-car companies offer special deals and discount coupons. When you're booking your hotel or plane reservations, ask if there is a car tie-in. The Hawaii State Consumer Protection Office also suggests that on fly/drive deals, you ask (1) whether the company will honor a reservation rate if only larger cars are available when you arrive, and (2) whether only certain credit cards will be accepted. **Hertz, Avis, National,** and **Dollar** systems have tie-ins with Hawaiian Air; **Budget** ties in with Aloha Airlines.

During peak seasons—summer, Christmas vacation, and February—car reservations are necessary.

Rental agencies abound in and around the Honolulu Airport and in Waikiki. Often it is cheaper to rent in Waikiki than at the airport. Expect to pay around $35–$45 daily at the airport and $30–$40 in Waikiki, with lower rates at local budget companies. On Oahu, unlimited mileage is often the rule. At press time, Dollar had the best daily rate and Budget the best weekly rate.

Avis (tel. 800/331–1212), **Hertz** (tel. 800/654–3131), **Budget** (tel. 800/527–0700), **Thrifty** (tel. 800/367–2277), **National** (tel. 800/328–4567), **Sears** (tel. 800/527–0770), and **Dollar** (tel. 800/421–6868) have airport and downtown offices. Local budget and used-rental-car companies include **Tropical** (tel. 808/836–1041), which serves other islands, too; **Roberts Hawaii** (tel. 808/947–3939), which will rent to married 18-year-olds; **Five-O** (tel. 808/695–5266), with special deals for members of the armed forces; **VIP** (tel. 808/946–1671); **Island World** (tel. 808/839–2222), another multi-island company.

Find out a few essentials *before* you arrive at the rental counter. (Otherwise a sales agent could talk you into additional costs you don't need.) The major added cost in renting cars is usually the so-called collision damage waiver (CDW). Find out from the rental agency you're planning to use what the waiver will cover. Your own employee or personal insurance may already cover the damage to a rental car. If so, bring along a photocopy of the benefits section of your insurance policy.

More and more companies—Hertz leading the way—now hold renters responsible for theft and vandalism if they don't buy the CDW. In response, some credit card and insurance companies are extending their coverage to rental cars. These include **Dreyfuss Bank Gold and Silver MasterCards** (tel. 800/847–9700), **Chase Manhattan Bank Visa Cards** (tel. 800/645–7352), and **Access America** (tel. 800/851–2800).

You should also find out before renting if you must pay for a full tank of gas whether you use it all or not. In addition, you should make sure the rental agency gives you a reservation number for the car you are planning to rent.

Staying in Waikiki

Important Addresses and Numbers

Hawaii Visitors Bureau 2270 Kalakaua Ave., 8th floor, Honolulu 96815, right in Waikiki, tel. 808/923–1811.

Emergencies 911 will get you the police, the fire department, an ambulance, or the suicide center.
Honolulu County Medical Society (tel. 808/536–6988)—information on doctors.
The Waikiki Drug Clinic (tel. 808/922–4787).
Coast Guard Rescue (tel. 808/536–4336).
Straub Walk-In Health Center. A doctor, laboratory/radiology technician, and nurses are on duty. No appointments are necessary. Services include diagnosis and treatment of illness and injury, laboratory testing and X-ray on site, and referral, when necessary, to Honolulu's Straub Hospital. More than 150 kinds of medical insurance are accepted, including Medicare, Medicaid, and most kinds of travel insurance. Sunburn care is a specialty. *Royal Hawaiian Shopping Center, 2233 Kalakaua Ave., Bldg. B, 3rd floor, tel. 808/971–6000. Clinic open weekdays 8:30–5:30. At other times, call the duty doctor at 808/926–4777.*

Pharmacies Both have the same ownership and advertise as sunburn specialists:

Outrigger Pharmacy (Outrigger Hotel, 2335 Kalakaua Ave., tel. 808/923–2529).
Kuhio Pharmacy (Outrigger West Hotel, 2330 Khuio Ave., tel. 923–4466).

Surf Report Dial 808/836–1952.

Weather Dial 808/836–0121.

Getting Around

Waikiki is only 2½ miles long and a half-mile wide. You can usually walk to where you are going. There are plenty of places to stop and rest, the shop windows are interesting, and people-watching is fun, and free.

Buses You can go all around the island or just down Kalakaua Avenue for 60¢ on Honolulu's municipal transportation system, affectionately known as The Bus (tel. 808/524–4626). You are also entitled to one free transfer per fare if you ask for it when boarding. Board at the front of the bus. Exact change is required. The student fare (grades 1–12) is 25¢ and children under 6 ride free. A free bus pass for senior citizens (age 65 or over and able to prove it) may be obtained by applying in person at 725 Kapiolani Blvd. between 8 AM and 4 PM, but it takes two to three weeks to be processed. Monthly bus passes are available at $15 for adults, $7.50 for students. In Waikiki, get them at Pioneer Federal Savings Bank, Waikiki Business Plaza, 2270 Kalakaua Ave.

There are no official bus-route maps, but you can find privately published booklets at most drugstores and other convenience outlets. The important route numbers for Waikiki are 2, 4, 5, 8, 19, and 20. If you venture afield, you can always get back on one of those.

There are also a number of brightly painted private buses, many free, that will take you to commercial attractions such as dinner cruises, garment factories, and the like.

Waikiki Trolley An open trolley cruises Waikiki, the Ala Moana area, and downtown, making 27 stops along a 90-minute route. The trolley ride provides a good orientation. The conductor narrates, pointing out sights, as well as shopping, dining, and entertainment opportunities along the way. *Tel. 808/526–0112. Buy an all-day pass from the conductor for $5 and for children under 12, $4. Daily 8 AM–5:45 PM.*

Taxis You can usually get one right at the doorstep of your hotel. Most restaurants will call a taxi for you. Rates are $1.40 at the drop of the flag, plus 20¢ for each additional ⅐ mile. Drivers are generally courteous and the cars in good condition, many of them air-conditioned. The two biggest taxicab companies are **Charley's,** a fleet of company-owned cabs (tel. 808/531–1333); and **SIDA of Hawaii, Inc.,** an association of individually owned cabs (tel. 808/836–0011).

Driving Your Mainland driver's license is valid in Hawaii for 90 days. If you're staying longer, apply for a Hawaii driver's license for $3 at the Honolulu Police Dept. Main Station, 1455 S. Beretania St., tel. 808/943–3111.

Be sure to buckle up. Hawaii has a seat-belt law for front-seat passengers. Children under age 3 must be in a car seat, available from your car-rental agency.

It's hard to get lost in Hawaii. Roads and streets, although they may be unpronounceable to the visitor (Kalanianaole Hwy., for example), are at least well marked. Major attractions and scenic spots are marked by the distinctive Hawaii Visitors Bureau sign with its red-caped warrior.

You can usually orient yourself by the mountains and the ocean. North, south, east, and west are less important than the local references. Go **mauka** means to go *toward the mountains* (north from Waikiki); go **makai** means to go *toward the ocean* (south); go toward **Diamond Head** means to go *in the direction of that famous landmark* (east); and go **ewa** (pronounced eva) means to go *away from Diamond Head* (west). You may be told that a shop is on the mauka–Diamond Head corner of the street, meaning it is on the mountain side of the street on the corner closest to Diamond Head. When giving directions, most local people state the highways by name, not by number.

Hawaii's drivers are generally courteous, and you rarely hear a horn. People will slow down and let you into traffic with a wave of the hand. A friendly wave back is appreciated and customary.

Driving in rush-hour traffic (6:30–8:30 AM and 3:30–5:30 PM) can be frustrating, not only because of the sheer volume of traffic but because left turns are forbidden at many intersections. Parking along many streets is curtailed during these hours, and towing is strictly enforced. Read the curbside parking signs before leaving your vehicle, even at a meter.

Don't leave valuables in your car. Tourists are targets for thieves because they probably won't be here by the time the case comes to trial, even if the crooks are caught.

Limos   **Roberts Hawaii** (tel. 808/973–2308) has Cadillacs for $55 an hour. **Silver Cloud Limousine Service** (tel. 808/524–7999) will provide red-carpet treatment and even private yachts and planes. A Mercedes 560 SL goes for $225 a day plus $35 for insurance.

Mopeds and Motorcycles   **Aloha Funway** (tel. 808/942–9696) has mopeds for $24.95 a day. Bicycles run from $12.95 a day.

Pedicabs   You may have heard about them, but they were recently banned, and no longer operate on the main streets. You may still find some cruising the side streets. Be sure to settle on the fare ahead of time, and don't buy anything else from the operator.

Guided Tours

Types of Tours   **Circle Island Tour.** There are several variations on this theme. Read Scenic Drives around Oahu in the Excursions from Waikiki chapter to decide what's important to you and then see which tour comes the closest to matching your desires. Some of these all-day tours include lunch. Cost: $35–$45, depending on whether lunch is included or whether you go by bus or minibus, the latter being slightly more expensive.

Little Circle Tour. These tours cover the territory discussed in the East Oahu Ring section of Scenic Drives around Oahu in the Excursions from Waikiki chapter. Most of these tours are the same, no matter what the company. This is a half-day tour. Cost: about $20.

Pearl Harbor, City and Punchbowl Tour. This comprehensive tour includes the boat tour to Pearl Harbor run by the National

Park Service. (*See* Sights around Oahu in Chapter 4 for particulars on the attractions.) Cost: about $20.

Polynesian Cultural Center. *See* Chapter 4 for details on the center. The only advantage of the tour is that you don't have to drive yourself back to Waikiki after dark if you take in the evening show. Cost: about $50–$60.

Tour Companies   Many "ground" companies handle these excursions. Some herd you onto an air-conditioned bus and others use smaller vans. Vans are recommended because less time is spent picking up passengers and you get to know your fellow passengers and your tour guide. Whether you go by bus or van, you'll probably be touring in top-of-the-line equipment. The competition among these companies is fierce, and everyone has to keep up. If you're booking through your hotel travel desk, ask whether you'll be on a bus or a van and exactly what the tour includes in the way of actual "get-off-the-bus" stops and "window sights."

Most of the tour guides have been in the business for years. Many have taken special Hawaiiana classes to learn their history and lore. They expect a tip ($1 per person at least), but they're just as cordial without one.

There are many tour companies. Here are some of the most reliable and popular:

American Express (tel. 808/924–6555). American Express books through several tour companies and can help you choose which tour best suits your needs.
Gray Line Hawaii (tel. 808/834–1033).
Diamond Head Tours (tel. 808/922–0544). Guides must complete the Bishop Museum's Hawaiiana classes.
E Noa Tours (tel. 808/599–2561). This company uses vans exclusively and likes to get you into the outdoors. On one of its Circle Island Tours you get to swim at Hanauma Bay.
Polynesian Adventure Tours (tel. 808/922–0888). Some tours are action-oriented.
Roberts Hawaii (tel. 808/947–3939).
Trans Hawaiian Services (tel. 808/735-6467 or 800/533–8765). Guide "Uncle Joe" Kalahiki is considered by both tourism professionals and returning visitors to be the king of guides.

Walking Tours   **Chinatown Walking Tour.** Meet at the Chinese Chamber of Commerce (42 N. King St.) for a fascinating peek into herbal shops, an acupuncturist's office, and specialty stores. The tour is sponsored by the Chinese Chamber of Commerce. Reservations required. *Tel. 808/533–3181. Cost: $4; add $5 to include lunch in a Chinese restaurant. Tues. only.*
"Historic Downtown Walking Tour." Volunteers from the Mission Houses Museum (553 S. King St.) take you on a two-hour walk through Honolulu, where the historic sites are side by side with the modern business towers. If it's Friday, end the tour by picking up a fast-food lunch and enjoying the noontime concert on the Iolani Palace lawn. *Tel. 808/531–0481. Reservations required. Cost: $7. Open weekdays.*
Clean Air Walks. Volunteers from this environmental action group conduct a variety of interesting walks, such as the "Wealthy Neighborhood Walk," the "Ala Moana Waterfront Walk," and a Diamond Head summit hike. Call for schedule. *Tel. 808/944–0804. Donation: $3–$5 to the Clean Air Fund. Fri. 9 AM.*

Great Outdoor Tours

Action Hawaii Adventures. This company manages to compress into one day adventures the tourist rarely gets to do in a week. You'll go on guided hikes through rain forests and valleys, swim beneath waterfalls, and snorkel at "insider" spots. Boogie-boarding and spearfishing are also available. A sandwich lunch plus samples of local food are included in the all-day tours. *Tel. 808/944–6754. Cost: $25–$65.*

Windward Expeditions. The guides know their history and lore as they take you by inflatable boat along the southeastern shore of Oahu. The hour-and-a-half excursion includes snorkeling and exploration of sea caves. Twenty-foot Zodiacs are the vessels. *Tel. 808/263–3899. Cost: $35.*

Helicopter Tours

Papillon. People always think of helicopter rides as expensive, and they can be. But if you've never tried the whirlybird, this company has a 10- to 12- minute bird's-eye introductory view of Waikiki and Diamond Head for $45. The 30-minute flight for $99 through the Nuuanu Pali is beautiful, or you can circle the island for one hour for $187. One tour even goes to Molokai for lunch. Called the Oahu–Molokai Odyssey, it costs $275. Best of all, these helicopters take off from a pad right by the Ilikai, so you don't have to bother with the confusion of airport traffic. *Discovery Bay, 1778 Ala Moana Blvd., tel. 808/836–1566.*

Flightseeing Tours

Aloha IslandAir has a new "flightseeing" tour of six Hawaiian islands—Oahu, Molokai, Lanai, Maui, Kahoolawe, and the Big Island of Hawaii. The full-day tour is aboard a de Havilland Dash-6 aircraft equipped with individual headsets and excellent viewing windows. Land tours are conducted at Parker Ranch, largest privately owned ranch in the United States; Lahaina on Maui, and Kalaupapa on Molokai, site of the Hansen's disease (leprosy) settlement where Father Damien labored and died. The $220 charge per person includes tour, lunch, group photo, Continental breakfast, and Waikiki pickup at 6 AM. *Commuter Terminal, Honolulu International Airport, tel. 800/323–3345 or 833–3219.*

2 Portraits of Waikiki

Hawaii at a Glance: A Chronology

c. AD 500 First human beings set foot on Hawaiian shores: Polynesians travel 2,000 miles in 60- to 80-foot canoes to the islands they name *Havaiki*, after their legendary homeland.

c. 1750 Birth of King Kamehameha.

1778 January: HMS *Resolution* and *Discovery*, captained by James Cook, land on Kauai; first Western encounter with Hawaii, which was not on any known Western map. Cook names the islands the Sandwich Islands after his patron, the Earl of Sandwich. November: Cook returns to Hawaii for the winter, anchors at Kealakekua Bay, on the Big Island.

1779 February: Cook is killed in a battle with indigenous people.

1786 Fur traders spend the winter in Hawaii; this becomes commonplace. Kamehameha consolidates his rule over the Big Island and attempts to extend his power over the other islands.

1790 First Westerners settle on islands.

1791 Kamehameha builds Puukohola Heiau temple; dedicates it by killing a rival chief.

1794 Kamehameha uses Western arms to complete his conquest of the islands.

1810 Chief of Kauai acknowledges Kamehameha's rule, uniting the islands under one chief.

1819 Death of Kamehameha; first whaling ships land at Lahaina on Maui.

1820 First missionaries arrive from Boston.

1835 First commercial sugar plantation on Kauai, financed by Americans.

1840 The Wilkes Expedition, sponsored by the U.S. Coast and Geodetic Survey, pinpoints Pearl Harbor as a potential naval base.

1852 Depopulation owing to Western diseases creates labor shortage; Chinese laborers brought in to work cane fields. They are followed by Portuguese, Japanese, Koreans, and Filipinos.

1863 Queen Emma, half-Caucasian widow of King Kamehameha IV, attempts to succeed her husband to the throne, but the Hawaiian legislature elects Chief David Kalakaua king.

1875   Treaty with United States establishes virtual protector-ate, gives sugar planters trade protection.

1882   King David Kalakaua builds Iolani Palace on the site of the previous royal palace, after a visit to the United States.

1887   Treaty with United States renewed; grants United States exclusive use of Pearl Harbor.

1891–93   Reign of Queen Liliuokalani. She is removed from throne by American business interests led by Sanford B. Dole (son of a missionary), and imprisoned in Iolani Palace.

1898   Hawaii annexed by United States.

1900   Pineapples become a profitable crop.

1901   First major tourist hotel, the Moana (now called the Shera-ton Moana Surfrider), built on Waikiki Beach.

1907   Fort Shafter Army Base built; first U.S. military post.

1908   Construction of base begins at Pearl harbor.

1919   Pearl Harbor dedicated.

1927   Matson Navigation Company builds Royal Hawaiian Hotel as destination for its cruise ships.

1941   Pearl Harbor bombed by Japanese, causing United States to enter World War II.

1942   James Jones, with thousands of others, trains at Schofield Barracks on Oahu. He later writes about it in *From Here to Eternity*.

1959   Hawaii granted statehood. Later in the year, the first Boe-ing 707 jets make the flight from San Francisco in five hours; tourism greatly increases, becoming Hawaii's major industry.

Diamond Head Inside Out

by Betty
Fullard-Leo

A journalist who
lives in Oahu,
Betty
Fullard-Leo is
Associate Editor
of ALOHA, The
Magazine of
Hawaii and the
Pacific.

The trail inside Diamond Head ambles off sedately enough from a green oasis irrigated into existence for Diamond Head State Park. It is later that the Sunday hiker, after crossing the open space of an old military target range, climbing the switchbacks, and blindly navigating a long, dark tunnel, becomes aware of a brooding sense of history in the ancient lava walls of this famous landmark.

The going gets tougher, as well as more intriguing, with a climb up concrete steps at the end of the tunnel into a catacomb of concrete hallways and barred rooms. Knowledgeable hikers avoid the stairs by taking a gentle path at their base along the outer edge of the crater rim. The splendor of Oahu's southeast coastline is spread out in a buffet of vistas from atop a concrete bunker just below the summit.

Black Point, a spit of land that harbors some of Hawaii's most opulent homes, is easy to identify. The whale-shaped hump of land beyond is Koko Head Crater. Inland, the imposing horseshoe-shaped Koko Crater evokes images of the fiery origins of the Hawaiian Islands that burst from the sea in flames millions of years earlier.

The story of Diamond Head itself goes back to a catastrophic explosion that created the crater about 150,000 years ago, or perhaps the story begins even earlier when the lava peaks that form the Hawaiian chain edged their way above the surface of the ocean. Of the eight major islands, Kauai was the first to surface, four or five million years ago. With the movement of the great tectonic plates of land under the sea, it gradually drifted to the northwest. Oahu appeared next as two separate volcanos of different ages. The older Waianae Range is on the western side, while the younger Koolau Range that separates the windward and leeward sides of Oahu is some two-and-a-half million years old. Lava flows from the Koolau volcano spilled into the sea to form the central plateau that today connects the two mountain ranges of Oahu.

In geologic times, a group of thirty relatively recent eruptions called the Honolulu Volcanic Series created the most obvious landmarks around Honolulu. These are the cinder cones and craters of Punchbowl National Cemetery, Diamond Head, Hanauma Bay, Rabbit Island, and Koko Crater, among others.

Diamond Head is a tuff cone, a type of volcano formed when molten rock, working its way toward the surface of the

"Diamond Head Inside Out" first appeared in ALOHA, The Magazine of Hawaii and the Pacific. Reprinted with permission from Davick Publications.

earth, comes in contact with water-saturated rocks. Theories vary, but most geologists agree that about 150,000 years ago, Diamond Head burst into being in an explosion that sprayed fine brown ash and pulverized rock and coral up to two miles in the air. Northeast tradewinds blew the settling ash southwest to create Leahi Peak, ringed by a nearly perfect conical crater with an average height of 400 feet. Geologists theorize erosion has carved away as much as a quarter of a mile on Diamond Head's seaward side. To prevent further erosion inside the crater, signs warn today's hikers to stay on the trail, but it is in these eroded areas that the bits of white coral and brown ash that are compacted to layers of rock in the walls of the crater are visible.

Because of this erosion, calcite crystals commonly known as "Pele's tears" once lay about the base, causing British sailors to christen the volcano "Diamond" Head in the 19th century. The Hawaiians had always called it "Laeahi" or "Leahi," possibly reflecting their early practice of lighting signal fires on the summit to guide home their fishing canoes. "Lae" means headland while "ahi" means fire. Another popular explanation for the Hawaiian name interprets "lae" as forehead, while "ahi" means tuna. Glance at any yellow-fin tuna in the fishmarket, and the similarity between Diamond Head's familiar profile and that of the tuna is obvious. It was given its first English name in 1786 when Captain Nathaniel Portlock called it Point Rose in honor of the secretary of the British treasury, but the name didn't stick. At other times it was dubbed Diamond Hill and Conical Mountain.

Hawaiians had their own explanation for the formation of Diamond Head. They believed the fire goddess, Pele, and her sister, Hiiaka, were driven from their home by an older jealous sister, Namakaokahai. The two goddesses went to live first on Kauai, causing the eruption of Puu Ka Pele as evidence of their presence. Namakaokahai drove them to Oahu, but the sea put out their fire at Leahi, so they moved on to Molokai, to Maui, and finally came to reside on the Big Island of Hawaii, where Pele continues to show her spirit-presence in eruptions at Kilauea Volcano.

Diamond Head was a sacred mountain to the Hawaiians, who once had five heiaus, or places of worship, in the crater. The stone remains of only one still exist. Kapua Heiau and Kupalaha Heiau were near Kapiolani Park. Fragments of a remaining wall show Kapua Heiau was approximately 240 feet square. Two heiaus had special purposes. Ahi Heiau on the peak of Diamond Head was a shrine dedicated to the god of winds. It served as protection against the updrafts that might put out the guiding light. Pahu-a-Manu Heiau was specifically for fishermen and seamen. Located where today's lighthouse stands, the men could watch for schools of fish while their priests made offerings at the site.

The most important heiau was Papaenaena, which was visible from Waikiki during the 19th century. Located approximately where the Hawaii School for Girls now stands, it is thought to have been built by the Maui king Kahekili to commemorate his conquest of Oahu and to execute the king of Oahu on a heiau that hadn't been used for the execution of one of his own ancestors. Papaenaena Heiau was dedicated to the war god Kukailimoku. It was here that King Kamehameha the Great celebrated his victory over Kalanikupule, the king of Oahu, Maui, Molokai, and Lanai, after the battle at Nuunau Pali in 1795. The heiau again figured in history in 1804 when Kamehameha lost his battle to conquer Kauai. Temple priests recommended a 10-day tabu and sacrificed 400 pigs, 400 coconuts, 400 branches of plantains and three human victims to appease the gods.

An early visitor to the Islands, John B. Whitman, wrote of his visit to Papaenaena in 1814: "I watched an opportunity to enter it and perceived a quantity of bones and cocoa nut shells scattered about, and on one side there was a pile of human skulls reaching half way to the top of the wall. I afterwards learned the skulls and bones were the remains of victims sacrificed to the Etour (gods). The walls of this charnel house were decorated with skulls placed along the top at intervals of a foot with the face outward as if to warn the unwary of their doom if their feet encroached upon the sacred spot."

Upon the death of Kamehameha in 1819 and the destruction of the religious kapu system by his heirs, the heiaus were abandoned or destroyed.

Papaenaena's three terraces were demolished in 1856, and its stones were used for fencing and roadwork. Some of these paving stones still remain around Iolani Palace.

The next forty years were a relatively quiet time in Diamond Head's history. Horses grazed among the scrub brush in the interior. An alkaline sink covered a portion of the 175-acre floor. A few private homes were built beneath its slopes on the Waikiki side, and in the early 1890s, the first steel-frame lighthouse was constructed on the seaward side. This was replaced and equipped with the latest automatic electric equipment 27 years later.

The political climate in Hawaii deteriorated into turmoil, and on January 7, 1893, a group of annexationists, led by Honolulu's American population, took control of the principal government buildings. They proclaimed a provisional government and deposed the queen. By January 6, 1895, native rebels or royalists, who were dissatisfied with the new government and who felt that Queen Liliuokalani should be returned to her rightful position as ruler, staged a rebellion that included "The Battle of Diamond Head."

The royalists were armed with 288 repeating Winchester rifles and 100 pistols that had been ordered from San Francisco. On the afternoon of January 6, Sam Nowlein, commander of the household troops under Liliuokalani, gave word that rebels should assemble at Diamond Head at 2 AM the next morning, but some of the rebels misunderstood the order and began to assemble immediately. When the government forces realized what was happening, martial law was declared and the National Guard and Citizens' Guard organizations were called to duty. Company E of the National Guard went to quell the 150 armed men mobilizing on the slopes of Diamond Head. Robert Wilcox, their leader, ordered his men to retreat to a better position on the rim of the crater, and fighting commenced.

At the same time, Sam Nowlein was leading another group of rebels in a battle at Moiliili. Fighting at Diamond Head went on during the day but as night fell, the royalists under Wilcox fled to Manoa Valley. Within a week, all of the royalists had been captured and Queen Liliuokalani was arrested and placed in confinement. Before a special military commission 190 prisoners were tried; only six were acquitted. Some were sentenced to be executed, others to prison terms and fines, but Sanford Dole, president of the Republic of Hawaii, later reduced most of the sentences as being too severe. Even the revised sentences were never carried out and by the time the United States annexed the Islands in 1898, all the prisoners had been pardoned.

In 1904 the United States government bought 729 acres around the crater for $3,300 at the recommendation of Major William E. Birkhimer. Assuming it could be found, a 100,000-square-foot lot for sale on Diamond Head today (granted it would probably have a house on it) might run anywhere from $350,000 to more than $1,000,000.

For 44 years the military closed Diamond Head crater to the public. Bunkers, gun mounts, battery and storage tunnels, observation posts, and communications rooms were constructed prior to World War II. A cable car lifted men and supplies from the crater floor to the west wall. During the war years, hundreds of soldiers occupied barracks in the crater. The existing trail was built between 1908 and 1910, but in the 1940s, camouflage nets hung like giant spider webs from high metal posts to hide traffic on the trail from curious eyes. Activities inside the crater were classified information.

Hikers in the crater today can still see the metal posts along the trail and can enter the concrete "lookouts" for sightseeing on five levels. Each level commands a different view of Oahu's coastline from the lowest "Station Able," with its windows focused southeast, to the top "Station

Easy," which looks to the west toward Pearl Harbor. It's only a short walk up a more recently installed metal staircase to the 763-foot Leahi summit. Swimming pools shine like giant blue sapphires in the Diamond Head residential area below, the pink Royal Hawaiian Hotel is dwarfed by Waikiki's high rises, and, farther up the coast to the west are the concrete ribbons that are Honolulu Airport's reef runway shimmering in the heat. Beyond is Pearl Harbor. The view is spectacular.

The return hike wends through a series of stairways and halls that connect the five lookout stations. A feeling of history and secrecy brings to mind the years when Diamond Head, with its fortifications, was known as the "Gibraltar of the Pacific." These underground rooms have prison-like bars, not because they housed fugitives, but because they held secret codes that had to remain under lock and key. The bars allowed air to circulate better than solid walls and doors.

The guns on Diamond Head were never used in war, and in 1950 the Army removed its paraphernalia and turned its facilities over to the Hawaii National Guard. Birkhimer Tunnel, a 14,728-square-foot room dug into the northeastern side of the crater, is used today by Hawaii's Civil Defense organization.

In 1955 and 1958 the Territory of Hawaii and the Federal Aviation Agency were given the land for defense and for air traffic control. A two-story green building in the crater now houses the FAA Center which directs the flight of approaching and departing planes when they are not in contact with the tower at the Honolulu International Airport.

Diamond Head was designated a national monument in 1968. Since then, it has attracted more and more visitors, even though tour operators are not allowed to conduct tours in Hawaii's public parks. Whatever the future holds for Diamond Head, it's a good bet that in some form it will stand sentinel over Hawaii's history and the resort area of Waikiki for years to come.

The Aloha Shirt: A Colorful Swatch of Island History

by DeSoto Brown

A fourth-generation Islander of part-Hawaiian ancestry, DeSoto Brown is the author of two books, Hawaii Recalls *and* Aloha Waikiki.

Elvis Presley had an entire wardrobe of them in the '60s films *Blue Hawaii* and *Paradise, Hawaiian Style.* During the '50s, entertainer Arthur Godfrey and bandleader Harry Owens often sported them on television shows. John Wayne loved to lounge around in them. Mick Jagger felt compelled to buy one on a visit to Hawaii in the 1970s. Dustin Hoffman, Steven Spielberg and Bill Cosby avidly collect them.

From gaudy to grand, from tawdry to tasteful, aloha shirts are Hawaii's gift to the world of fashion. It's been more than 50 years since those riotously colored garments made their first appearance as immediately recognizable symbols of the Islands.

The roots of the aloha shirt go back to the early 1930s, when Hawaii's garment industry was just beginning to develop its own unique style. Although locally made clothes did exist, they were almost exclusively items for plantation workers, which were constructed of durable palaka or plain cotton material.

Out of this came the first stirrings of fashion: Beachboys and schoolchildren started having sport shirts made from colorful Japanese kimono fabric. The favored type of cloth was the kind used for children's kimonos—bright pink and orange floral prints for girls; masculine motifs in browns and blues for boys. In Japan, such flamboyant patterns were considered unsuitable for adult clothing, but in the Islands, such rules didn't apply, and it seemed the flashier the shirt, the better—for either sex. Thus, the aloha shirt was born.

It was easy and inexpensive in those days to have garments tailored to order; the next step was moving to mass production and marketing. In June 1935, Honolulu's best-known tailoring establishment, Musa-Shiya, advertised the availability of "Aloha shirts—well tailored, beautiful designs and radiant colors. Ready-made or made to order . . . 95¢ and up." This is the first known printed use of the term that would soon refer to an entire industry. By the following year, several local manufacturers had begun full-scale production of "aloha wear." One of them, Ellery Chun of King-Smith, registered as local trademarks the terms "Aloha

"The Aloha Shirt: A Colorful Swatch of Island History" first appeared in ALOHA, The Magazine of Hawaii and the Pacific. *Reprinted with permission of Davick Publications.*

Sportswear" and "Aloha Shirt" in 1936 and 1937, respectively.

These early entrepreneurs were the first to create uniquely Hawaiian designs for fabric as well—splashy patterns that would forever symbolize the Islands. A 1939 *Honolulu Advertiser* story described them as a "delightful confusion (of) tropical fish and palm trees, Diamond Head and the Aloha Tower, surfboards and leis, ukuleles and Waikiki beach scenes."

The aloha wear of the late 1930s was intended for—and mostly worn by—tourists, and interestingly, a great deal of it was exported to the Mainland and even Europe and Australia. By the end of the decade, for example, only 5% of the output of one local firm, the Kamehameha Garment Company, was sold in Hawaii.

World War II brought this trend to a halt, and during the postwar period, aloha wear really came into its own in Hawaii. A strong push to support local industry gradually nudged Island garb into the workplace, and kamaainas began to wear the clothing that previously had been seen as attire for visitors.

In 1947, for example, male employees of the City and County of Honolulu were first allowed to wear aloha shirts "in plain shades" during the summer months. Later that year, the first observance of Aloha Week started the tradition of "bankers and bellhops . . . mix(ing) colorfully in multi-hued and tapa-designed Aloha shirts every day," as a local newspaper's Sunday magazine supplement noted in 1948. By the 1960s, "Aloha Friday," set aside specifically for the wearing of aloha attire, had become a tradition. In the following decade, the suit and tie practically disappeared as work attire in Hawaii, even for executives.

Most of the Hawaiian-themed fabric used in manufacturing aloha wear was designed in the Islands then printed on the Mainland or in Japan. The glowingly vibrant rayons of the late '40s and early '50s (a period now seen as aloha wear's heyday) were at first printed on the East Coast, but manufacturers there usually required such large orders, local firms eventually found it impossible to continue using them. By 1964, 90% of Hawaiian fabric was being manufactured in Japan—a situation that still exists today.

Fashion trends usually move in cycles, and aloha wear is no exception. By the 1960s, the "chop suey print" with its "tired clichés of Diamond Head, Aloha Tower, outrigger canoes (and) stereotyped leis" was seen as corny and garish according to an article published in the *Honolulu Star Bulletin*. But it was just that outdated aspect that began to appeal to the younger crowd, who began searching out old-fashioned aloha shirts at the Salvation Army and Goodwill thrift stores. These shirts were dubbed "silkies," a name by which they're still known, even though most of them were actually made of rayon.

Before long, what had been 50-cent shirts began escalating in price, and a customer who had balked at paying $5 for a shirt that someone had already worn soon found the same item selling for $10—and more. By the late 1970s, aloha wear designers were copying the prints of yesteryear for their new creations.

The days of bargain silkies are now gone. The few choice aloha shirts from decades past that still remain are offered today by specialized dealers for hundreds of dollars apiece, causing many to look back with chagrin to the time when such treasures were foolishly worn to the beach until they fell apart. The best examples of vintage aloha shirts are now rightly seen as art objects worthy of preservation for the lovely depictions they offer of Hawaii's colorful and unique scene.

Hawaii's History

Hawaii's chain of volcanic islands, blessed by sunshine, soft winds, and jagged green mountains, rises out of a lonely stretch of the North Pacific, thousands of miles from land. No one knows exactly when these islands were first inhabited. Although it was originally believed that the first people arrived in the 11th century, new evidence indicates that they arrived about 500 years earlier.

The exact identification of these first settlers is also unclear. Most researchers believe they were people originally from Southeast Asia who discovered the South Pacific islands of Tahiti and the Marquesas. The most prevalent theory is that they probably came from the Marquesas, now part of French Polynesia. Even why they ended up in Hawaii is open to debate.

One thing is certain: This string of islands was settled by seafaring people whose seamanship had already taken them to many islands in the vast southern and eastern expanses of the Pacific. The staggering proportions of their feats can be fully appreciated only if one considers that they sailed across 2,000 miles of open ocean centuries before the Vikings left Europe's shores and more than 1,000 years before the first voyage of Columbus. It's not even known what these people called themselves. The original inhabitants of Hawaii were named Polynesians by Europeans. Polynesia means "many islands" in Greek and refers to the oceanic realm of the South Pacific.

If settlers did indeed first set foot on Hawaii in the 6th century, it would be nearly 1,300 years later before the first European laid eyes on these islands. Captain James Cook, an Englishman, first sighted the island of Oahu on January 18, 1778, and "discovered" it for the Western world.

Captain Cook, commander of the HMS *Resolution* and the consort vessel HMS *Discovery*, was already known as England's greatest explorer of the world's uncharted oceans. Cook had discovered dozens of South Pacific islands on two previous voyages. On his third venture into the Pacific, he was going north of the equator into the uncharted North Pacific, in search of the legendary Northwest Passage, believed to be a seaway link between the Pacific and the Atlantic. After spending Christmas Day on an atoll north of Tahiti, which he named Christmas Island, he set sail for the top of the North American continent. He did not expect to see land again until he had crossed nearly 3,000 miles of ocean.

But just 16 days later, Cook and all hands were on deck, gazing in wonder as they saw the mountains of the Hawaiian Islands looming in the distance through the predawn mist. They were even more astonished when they saw people in canoes rowing toward them from the shore.

Cook stepped ashore onto the island of Kauai, the first of the Islands he was to visit. He named the archipelago the Sandwich Islands, for the Earl of Sandwich, his patron. In 1779 Cook was killed in a fight with Hawaiians at Kealakekua on the island of Hawaii.

The splendid isolation of the Islands ended abruptly after Cook's arrival. First came British explorers, then came British, American, French, and Russian traders. Whalers from New England soon followed. Tales spread of thousands of acres of sugarcane growing wild, and the farmers came in droves, from the United States and Europe.

At the time of Cook's arrival, each island was ruled as an independent kingdom by hereditary chiefs, who often warred among themselves. One such chief was Kamehameha, who was the first to unify the Islands. He began his rise to power in 1790 through a series of bloody battles to unify the island of Hawaii. He then went on to conquer Maui and Oahu. By the time of his death in 1819, he was King Kamehameha I, ruling the unified Kingdom of Hawaii with an iron hand. Hawaii had a total of seven monarchs, four of them descendants of Kamehameha I. The Islands would remain a monarchy until 1893, when Queen Liliuokalani, the last of Hawaii's monarchs, was deposed during a bloodless revolution that led to a provisional government headed by an American, Sanford Ballard Dole. He proclaimed himself president of the Republic of Hawaii in 1894.

One of the pivotal years in Hawaiian history was 1820, the year the first missionaries arrived from New England. At this time, King Kamehameha I had only been dead one year, yet already the social order was beginning to break down. The Hawaiians were disillusioned with their own gods and were receptive to the ideas of Christianity. The influx of Western culture had also brought the introduction of Western diseases, liquor, and what some viewed as moral decay. The missionaries gained great success because they aligned themselves with the chiefs against some of the evils linked to the Westerners.

The second king to reign was Kamehameha II, the eldest of two sons of the first king. His short reign was noted for the official demise of the pagan religion, which included human sacrifice, and the breakdown of ancient taboos, such as the taboo against women eating with men, something which for centuries had been punishable by death. King Kamehameha II and his queen died of measles in 1824.

His younger brother became King Kamehameha III, a wise and gentle sovereign who ruled for 30 years. King Kamehameha III turned Hawaii into a constitutional monarchy in 1849, and won official recognition of Hawaii as an independent country by the United States, France, and Great Britain. In 1845 the King and the Legislature moved the seat of government from Lahaina, on Maui, to Honolulu, on Oahu. His other many notable accomplishments include the opening of Maui's Lahainaluna School, the oldest high school west of the Rocky Mountains; the establishment of the first permanent sugar plantation; and the publication of the first newspaper in the Pacific area.

In the early 1850s, toward the end of King Kamehameha III's reign, Hawaii's legendary ethnic diversity began in earnest, driven by labor shortages in the sugarcane fields. Between 1852 and 1946 a steady stream of foreign labor poured into Hawaii. The first to arrive were the Chinese, brought in by contract, to work on the sugarcane plantations. The Japanese began arriving in 1868, and later came Filipinos, Koreans, Portuguese, and Puerto Ricans.

The importance of sugar in Hawaii's political and economic history cannot be overstated. American merchants in Honolulu financed the first commercial sugar plantation on Kauai in 1835. Plantations soon sprouted on Oahu, Maui, and the island of Hawaii. By the end of the 19th century, sugar was "king" and Hawaii's only major export. As the importance of sugar in the local economy grew, the plantation owners began looking toward annexation with the United States as a means of establishing a firm market for their product. But the monarchs did not support annexation.

Kamehameha IV and V, grandsons of the first king, ruled about eight years each. With the death in 1872 of Kamehameha V, the line of direct descendents of the first king ended. A series of power struggles ensued between the adherents of David Kalakaua, who was elected by the Hawaii Legislature, and supporters of the Dowager Queen Emma, widow of Kamehameha IV. American and British marines were called in to restore order.

King Kalakaua reigned from 1874 through 1891, a turbulent period in which he battled for an increase in the personal authority of the king and dreamed of a Polynesian empire. It was during his reign that the United States and Hawaii signed a treaty of reciprocity in 1875, assuring Hawaii a duty-free market for sugar in the United States. The treaty's renewal in 1887 gave the United States the exclusive use of Pearl Harbor as a coaling station. Hawaii's strategic importance as a naval base was recognized as early as 1840 when the first U.S. survey of the Hawaiian Islands singled out Pearl Harbor as having enormous potential for harboring warships.

King Kalakaua, who died in 1891 during a visit to San Francisco, was succeeded by his sister, Liliuokalani, the last monarch of Hawaii. She unwittingly opened the door to efforts of the sugar barons to annex Hawaii to the United States. In trying to eliminate the restrictions that had been placed on the monarchy, Queen Liliuokalani brought on a bloodless revolution and was deposed after reigning only two years.

Sanford Ballard Dole, who formed a provisional government, requested Hawaii's annexation by the United States, but President Grover Cleveland refused. As a result, the provisional government converted Hawaii into a republic and proclaimed Dole president in 1894. The outbreak of the Spanish-American War in 1898 and Hawaii's strategic military importance in the Pacific led the next U.S. president, William McKinley, to look toward annexation with a more sympathetic eye. On August 12, 1898, Hawaii was officially annexed, by a joint resolution of Congress. Sanford Dole was appointed first governor of the territory on February 20, 1901.

A cousin of Sanford Dole, James D. Dole, developed the pineapple industry in Hawaii. This cousin was a New Englander who experimented with pineapples until he found a variety that would grow successfully in the Islands. In 1903 he made his first canned pineapple pack, producing nearly 2,000 cases. This marked the beginning of Hawaii's great pineapple industry, which today is much more prominent than its sugar industry.

In the early 1900s, Hawaii's military industry also gained importance. In 1907 Fort Shafter, headquarters for the U.S. Army, became the first permanent military post in the islands. Dredging of the channel at Pearl Harbor began in 1908. Formally dedicated by the U.S. Navy in 1919, Pearl Harbor would become a tragic part of U.S. history on December 7, 1941, when the U.S. Pacific Fleet was attacked by the Japanese. Nearly 4,000 casualties resulted from that surprise attack. Today, Pearl Harbor and the USS *Arizona* Memorial are among Hawaii's major tourist attractions.

In the 1920s Hawaiians began to increase efforts to promote tourism, the industry that would eventually dominate development of the Islands. In 1927 Army Lieutenants Lester Maitland and Albert Hegenberger made the first successful nonstop flight from the mainland. Commercial interisland air service began two years later. In 1936 Pan American World Airways made history as the first to start regular commercial passenger flights to Hawaii from the Mainland.

The year Hawaii gained statehood, 1959, was a major turning point in the history of the Islands for yet another reason: the first Boeing 707 jet planes arrived, flying from California to Honolulu in a record five hours. That same year, 243,216 tourists visited Hawaii. Today tourism is Hawaii's largest industry, drawing more than 5 million visitors a year.

While Hawaii's sugar, pineapple, military, and tourist industries were growing, the dream of statehood grew stronger. The campaign for statehood began at the turn of the century, with the overthrow of the last monarch. The road to statehood was a slow one, an acrimonious struggle taking more than half a century. Racism was blamed for many of the problems. Hawaii's great racial diversity did not sit well with some conservative members of Congress who resisted the idea of statehood for a territory that was heavily non-Caucasian. Anti-Japanese sentiment following the attack on Pearl Harbor further fueled the debate. But Hawaiians persevered, and on March 12, 1959, Congress passed legislation admitting Hawaii into the Union. Hawaii officially became the 50th state on Admission Day, August 21, 1959.

Hawaii's royal history may be rediscovered on Oahu, not far from Waikiki. The Iolani Palace, located in downtown Honolulu, is an elaborately restored, four-story Italian Renaissance structure, built in 1882 by the last Hawaiian king, David Kalakaua. It was here also that Queen Liliuokalani, the last reigning monarch, was deposed and imprisoned for nearly eight months by American businessmen who wanted Hawaii annexed to the United States.

Another royal treasure is Queen Emma Summer Palace, once the home of Kamehameha IV's wife. Now a museum, this palace recalls a history of misfortune that plagued Queen Emma, who, in her late twenties, suffered the death of her infant son Prince Albert and Kamehameha IV within 15 months of each other. She then tried and failed to succeed her husband to the throne.

Hawaii has been careful to preserve its history, especially its ancient history. Much of this past is found on the land itself rather than in old buildings; ancient burial caves, royal fish ponds, and petroglyph fields are likely to be found alongside of seaside resorts. State and federal laws have made archaeology in Hawaii a priority. An archaeological site investigation is required before any new construction can begin. This not only protects what already exists, but it has often led to new revelations about when the Islands were first inhabited.

3 Exploring Waikiki

Walking Tours of Waikiki

It's usually too sunny, too beautiful, and too warm to spend an entire day walking around Waikiki, no matter how interesting the sights may be. The three walks described here take you from one end of Waikiki to the other. You can try one walk a day sandwiched between time at the beach or you could do all three in one day. Some of the sights are a bit off the beaten track, not in terms of distance but in terms of what's been hyped.

Directions in the area are often given as:

mauka—toward the mountains (north); **makai**—toward the ocean (south); **Diamond Head**—toward Diamond Head (east); and **ewa**—away from Diamond Head (west).

You'll find these terms used in this chapter and the following chapter, Excursions from Waikiki.

Numbers in the margin correspond with points of interest on the Waikiki map.

Tour 1

❶ The **Ilikai Waikiki Hotel** (1777 Ala Moana Blvd.) is a good place to start a walking tour. From the second-floor pool deck,
❷ there's a good view of the **Ala Wai Yacht Harbor,** home berth to an armada of pleasure boats and two yacht clubs, both of which are open to members only. America's Cup champion skipper Dennis Conner hung his binnacle at the Waikiki Yacht Club when training for his victorious race against the Australians in 1987. It's fun to ride the Ilikai Waikiki's glass elevator, but it doesn't start running until 5:30 PM. From Annabelle's lounge at the top, the views of the sunset are spectacular, and you can see the whole of Waikiki stretching toward Diamond Head.

Head toward the main intersection of Ala Moana Boulevard and
❸ Kalia Road. Take a little detour to the **Rainbow Bazaar** shopping center in the **Hilton Hawaiian Village** (2005 Kalia Rd.). The Rainbow Bazaar is an elegant hodgepodge of Asian architecture, with a Chinese moon gate and pagoda and a Japanese farmhouse with a water wheel, all dominated by the tall mosaic mural of the Rainbow Tower. This is a good place to snap some pictures.

Stroll through the lavish gardens and look for the penguin pond in back of the main lobby. The hotel fronts the pretty Kahanamoku Lagoon and beach. It looks like the quintessential tropical lagoon, complete with a little island and palm trees.

❹ Across the street on Kalia Road is the U.S. Army's **Fort DeRussy.** On Saturday evenings during the summer, there are Catholic Masses on the lawn by the beach, with the setting sun as a backdrop and a lot of Hawaiian pageantry as part of the service. (For the schedule, tel. 808/263–8844.) Battery Randolf (Building 32) was built in 1909 as a key in the defense of Pearl Harbor and Honolulu. Within its walls, which measure 22 feet thick in places, is the **Army Museum,** housing an intimidating collection of war paraphernalia. The major focus is World War II memorabilia, but exhibits range from ancient Hawaiian weaponry to displays relating to the Vietnam War. *Tel. 808/438–2821. Group guided tours can be arranged. Admission free. Open 10 AM–4:30 PM; closed Mon.*

Across the street from Fort DeRussy, at 245 Saratoga Rd.,
nestled snugly amid the commerce of Waikiki, is an oasis of
tranquility: the **Tea House of the Urasenke Foundation.** Take
part in a Japanese tea ceremony; you'll be served tea and
sweets by ladies in kimonos. The Urasenke Foundation is a
centuries-old institution based in Kyoto, Japan. It has set the
etiquette for the tea ceremony based on the Zen philosophy
that has influenced Japanese art and taste. The Waikiki teahouse was donated by the Kyoto foundation and was the first to
be built outside Japan. The teahouse is a good, basic introduction to Japanese culture. Wear something comfortable (but no
shorts, please) for sitting on the floor. *Tel. 808/923–3059. Open
Wed. and Fri., 10* AM. Minimum donation: $2.

With a little zip from the tea and a little Zen for the road, head
mauka (toward the mountains, north) toward Kalakaua Avenue and turn toward Diamond Head. At **First Hawaiian Bank**
(2181 Kalakaua Ave.) on the corner of Lewers Street, look in
the lobby for six massive murals; these paintings depict the
populating of Hawaii. They also deal with the evolution of Hawaiian culture—from Hawaiian arts before contact with the
Western world to the introduction of the first printing press to
the Islands in 1872. The impressive panels were painted by the
late Jean Charlot, whose work is represented in the Uffizi Gallery in Florence, the British Museum in London, and the
Metropolitan Museum and the Museum of Modern Art in New
York. The murals are beautifully lit at night, with some panels
visible from the street.

Across the street, at 2200 Kalakaua Avenue, is one of Waikiki's
architectural landmarks, the blue-tile roof of the **Gump Building.** Built in 1929, it was once the premier store of Hawaii and
was known for the quality of its Asian and Hawaiian objects.
Now it houses a Crazy Shirts T-shirt shop and a McDonald's.

Walk down Lewers Street toward the ocean, to the impressive
Halekulani Hotel (2199 Kalia Rd.). The most interesting thing
about the hotel, aside from its famed restaurants, is the gigantic floral arrangement in the lobby. While you're there, take a
peek at the swimming pool with its huge orchid mosaic at the
bottom. Incorporated into the relatively new Halekulani Hotel
is a portion of its old (1917) structure, which was the setting for
the first of the Charlie Chan detective novels, *The House without a Key.*

Time Out If it's lunchtime, you should enjoy dining at **Orchids** restaurant
in the Halekulani with a view of Diamond Head from every ta-
ble. The lunch menu includes light entrées and tasty salads.
But if you're looking for eye-boggling quantity, wait a few minutes until you reach the **Royal Hawaiian Hotel** and try its
famous lunch buffet in the Surf Room, $15.75, served daily
noon–2:30 PM.

From the Halekulani, treat yourself to a stroll along the ocean
on the paved walkway leading past the **Sheraton Waikiki** (2255
Kalakaua Ave.) to the gracious old **Royal Hawaiian Hotel** (2259
Kalakaua Ave.). The lovely lobby, with its pink decor, is reminiscent of another era. A stroll through the old gardens, with
their tall swaying coconut palms and vivid flowers, is like step-
ping through a time warp to a period when Waikiki was a
sleepy, tropical paradise with a couple of gracious old hotels.

Waikiki

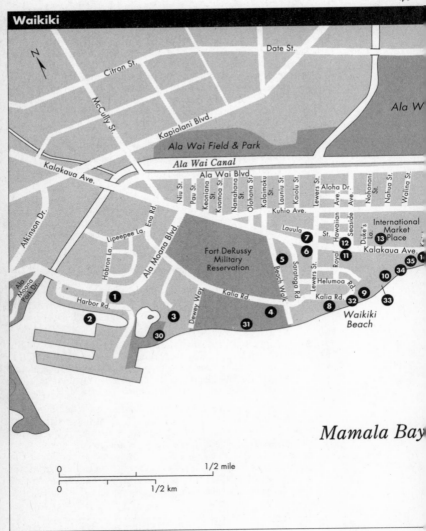

Date St.

Citron St.

McCully St.

Kapiolani Blvd.

Ala Wai Field & Park

Ala W

Kalakaua Ave.

Ala Wai Canal

Atkinson Dr.

Ala Wai Blvd.

Niu St.
Pau St.
Keoniana St.
Kuamoo St.
Namahana St.
Olohana St.
Kalaimoku St.
Launiu St.
Kaiolu St.
Lewers St.
Aloha Dr.
Nohononi St.
Nahua St.
Walina St.

Kuhio Ave.

Lipeepee La.
Ena Rd.

Ala Moana Blvd.

Lauula

7

St.
Royal Hawaiian Ave.
Seaside Ave.
Duke's la.

13 International Market Place

12

Kalakaua Ave.

1

6

11

Fort DeRussy Military Reservation

Beach Walk

Saratoga Rd.

5

Lewers St.

Helumoa Rd.

35

34

Hobron La.

Kalia Rd.

10

Kalia Rd.

9

8

32

33

Harbor Rd.

1

Dewey Way

4

Waikiki Beach

Ala Moana Park Dr.

2

3

31

30

Mamala Bay

0 — 1/2 mile

0 — 1/2 km

Walking Tours
Ala Wai Yacht
Harbor, **2**
Army Museum, Fort
De Russy, **4**
Damien Museum, **19**
Diamond Head, **29**
Diamond Head Hiking
Trail, **29**

First Hawaiian Bank,
Jean Charlot Murals, **6**
Fort De Russy, **4**
Gardens, Hilton
Hawaiian Village, **3**
Gardens, Royal
Hawaiian Hotel, **10**
Gump Building, **7**
Halekulani Hotel, **8**
Hawaii Visitors
Bureau, **12**

Hilton Hawaiian
Village, **3**
Honolulu Zoo, **20**
Hyatt Regency
Waikiki, **15**
Ilikai Waikiki Hotel, **1**
International Market
Place, **13**
Kahuna (or Wizard)
Stones, **16**

Kapiolani
Bandstand, **24**
Kapiolani Park, **21**
Kapiolani Park Rose
Garden, **28**
King's Village, **14**
Kodak Hula Show, **23**
New Otani Kaimana
Beach Hotel, **27**
Pacific Beach Hotel
Aquarium, **17**

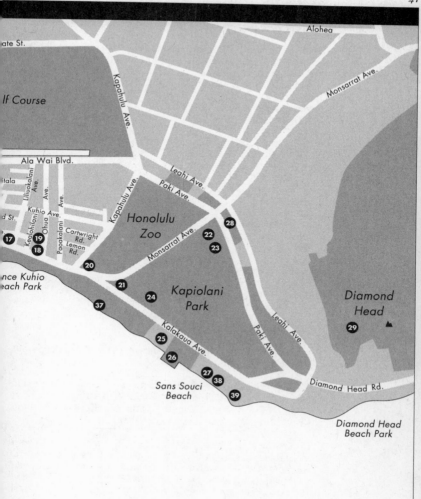

Rainbow Bazaar
Hilton Hawaiian
Village, **3**
Royal Hawaiian
Hotel, **10**
Royal Hawaiian
Shopping Center, **11**
St. Augustine's
Church, **18**
Sheraton Moana
Surfrider Hotel, **16**
Sheraton Waikiki, **9**

Tea House of the
Urasenke
Foundation, **5**
Waikiki Aquarium, **25**
Waikiki Business
Plaza, **12**
Waikiki Shell, **22**
Waikiki War Memorial
Natatorium, **26**
Zoo Fence Art
Mart, **20**

Beaches
Fort De Russy
Beach, **31**
Gray's Beach, **32**
Kahaloa Beach, **33**
Kahanamoku Beach
and Lagoon, **30**

Kuhio Beach Park, **36**
Outrigger Canoe
Club, Beach, **39**
Queen's Surf
Beach, **37**
Sans Souci Beach, **38**
Ulukou Beach, **34**
Waikiki Beach
Center, **35**

The illusion is only momentary, for the path leads to the ⑪ modern **Royal Hawaiian Shopping Center** (2201 Kalakaua Ave.). There are so many interesting shops tucked away here, it's a wonder that some of them are surviving, especially those on the upper floors (*see* Chapter 5).

Time Out A good treat to try while at the Royal Hawaiian mall is the local favorite, shave ice, the Hawaiian version of a snow cone, which comes in exotic fruit flavors like *lychee* and *li hing mui*. Have it with ice cream and *azuki* beans at the Island Snow stand.

Across the street from the Royal Hawaiian Shopping Center is ⑫ the **Waikiki Business Plaza** (2270 Kalakaua Ave.), recognizable by its fish mosaic mural and little fountain. The **Hawaii Visitors Bureau** (tel. 808/923–1811) is on the eighth floor. Pick up free booklets on hotels, buses, and restaurants, as well as a calendar of events. On the 10th floor are some wholesale fashion outlets open to the public. This is a good place to end a day's walking tour, or to take a break before moving on.

Tour 2

Begin this tour at the Waikiki Business Plaza. Walking toward Diamond Head, in the middle of the same block, you can't miss ⑬ the **International Market Place** (2330 Kalakaua Ave.) with its spreading banyan and Swiss Family Robinson–style tree-house. There's usually a lot of activity here, with wood-carvers, basket weavers, and other artisans from various Pacific islands creating and selling their handicrafts. Most of the souvenir stuff, both tacky and 24 karat, is sold from little Asian-style pushcarts.

Time Out The **Food Court** in the **Market Place** is a collection of individual food concessions with a central outdoor seating area. It includes inexpensive Japanese, Chinese, Korean, Filipino, Greek, Italian, and American kitchens.

If you can stand another shopping mall, turn mauka (toward ⑭ mountains, north) on Kaiulani Avenue to **King's Village** (131 Kaiulani Ave.). It's ultra-cute, with cobblestone streets and salespeople in period garb. There's a Burger King here, and you can sit outside under umbrellas. A Changing of the Guard ceremony is enacted every evening at 6:15, with "soldiers" in monarchy-era uniforms.

If you take a short walk from King's Village in the direction of ⑮ Diamond Head, you'll reach the **Hyatt Regency Waikiki** (2424 Kalakaua Ave.). To help visitors become acquainted with Hawaiian arts and crafts, Auntie Malia Solomon, resident Hawaiian authority for the Hyatt Regency, has assembled what she calls her "sharing place." The hotel calls the small second-floor museum of artifacts, quilts, and crafts **Hyatt's Hawaii**. It's a charming collection.

Time Out If you need to rest your feet, stop off at **Harry's Cafe and Bar**, which is right in the Hyatt Regency's atrium with a waterfall (on the ground floor). Harry's is a fun place to people-watch, and the inexpensive menu includes tasty sandwiches, homemade croissants, and other deli treats.

Across the way, the oldest hotel in Waikiki, the venerable **Moana,** has undergone a major historical renovation. Wander through the breezy lobby out to the wide back porch that looks out on the beach. They've done a beautiful job on this historic building. The Moana is now merged with the neighboring Surfrider Hotel and is renamed the **Sheraton Moana Surfrider** (2365 Kalakaua Ave.). There are period furnishings, historical exhibits, and plenty of nostalgia. The Beaux Arts–style hotel has been placed on the National Register of Historic Places. Visit the **Historical Room** in the Rotunda just above the main entrance, and enjoy a collection of old photographs and memorabilia dating from the opening of the hotel in 1901.

Next to the Sheraton Moana Surfrider are the four **Kahuna** (or **Wizard) Stones of Waikiki,** which, according to legend, were placed there in tribute to four prophets from Tahiti, who came to Hawaii sometime before the 16th century. Before disappearing, the prophets are said to have transferred their healing powers to the stones. They're by the beach showers, and, more often than not, are irreverently draped in wet towels.

Two blocks away at 2490 Kalakaua Avenue, with an entrance on Liliuokalani Avenue, is the **Pacific Beach Hotel,** with its huge 280,000-gallon aquarium. The aquarium is two stories high and harbors a thousand fish. The **Oceanarium Restaurant** is on the lobby level, and the hotel's fine dining room, **Neptune's,** is directly above it. Both wrap around the aquarium. *Tel. 808/922–1233. Admission free. Daily feeding times are 9 and 11:30 AM; 12:30, 5:30, 6:30, and 7:30 PM.*

If you walk two blocks toward Diamond Head, you'll find the only church in Waikiki with its own building, the Roman Catholic **Saint Augustine's** (130 Ohua Ave., tel. 808/923–7024). At press time, tempers were at a rolling boil due to the local bishop's decision to sell the church and its very valuable land to Japanese investors. Outraged clergy are appealing to Rome.

Just around the corner, in back of the church, is the **Damien Museum,** a small but fascinating two-room exhibit centering on the life and work of the Belgian priest Father Joseph Damien de Veuster, who came to Hawaii and labored and died among the victims of Hansen's disease (leprosy) on the island of Molokai. Ask to see the museum's 20-minute videotape. It is low-budget, but well done and emotionally gripping. *Tel. 808/923–2690. Admission free. Open weekdays, 9–3, Sat. 9–noon.*

With much to think about, this is another good place to end a tour of Waikiki. The area in and around Kapiolani Park, next on the list, is worth a day's outing by itself to allow plenty of time to smell the flowers—and the fresh clean surf.

Tour 3

Start this tour at the **Honolulu Zoo** (151 Kapahulu Ave., on the corner of Kalakaua Ave. and Kapahulu Ave.), which is just a two-block walk toward Diamond Head from the Damien Museum. The zoo is 40 green acres of lush foliage and home to 2,000 furry and finned creatures. There are bigger and better zoos, but this one is pretty, and where else can you see a *nene,* Hawaii's state bird? On Wednesday evenings in the summer, the zoo offers "The Wildest Show in Town," a free program of singing, dancing, and other entertainment. Check the local newspaper, either the *Honolulu Advertiser* or *Star Bulletin*, for what's playing. Pack a picnic supper (order it from your hotel, or *see* Picnics in Chapter 4), and join local families for a night out at the zoo. There is a new petting zoo and elephant show. *Tel. 808/971–7171. Admission: $1, children free. Open daily 8:30–4.*

Wednesdays, Saturdays, and Sundays, look for the **Zoo Fence Art Mart,** on Monsarrat Avenue outside the zoo, on the Diamond Head side. There's some affordable work by good contemporary artists that will make better souvenirs of Hawaii than some of the junky ashtrays and monkeypod Hawaiian gods carved in the Philippines.

㉑ ㉒ Across Monsarrat Avenue between Kalakaua Avenue and Paki Street, in **Kapiolani Park,** is the **Waikiki Shell,** Honolulu's outdoor concert arena. Check the newspaper to see what's playing. Local people bring a picnic and get "grass" seats (lawn seating). Here's a chance to have a magical night listening to some of the world's best musicians while lying on a blanket with the moon shining over Diamond Head.

㉓ In bleachers adjacent to the Waikiki Shell, the famous **Kodak Hula Show** has been wowing crowds for more than 50 years. It's colorful, lively, and fun. For the best seats, get there by 9:30 AM for the 10 AM one-hour show. Naturally, it's a great opportunity to take photographs. *Tel. 808/833–1661. Admission: $2.50. Shows Tues.–Thurs. only.*

㉔ Kapiolani Park's other major entertainment area is the **Kapiolani Bandstand.** There's usually a free show of some kind on Sunday afternoons at 2, frequently a concert by the Royal Hawaiian Band. Check the newspaper for particulars. Some excellent hula dances are performed here by local groups that don't frequent the hotels.

㉕ To save steps, cut diagonally across the park to the **Waikiki Aquarium** (2777 Kalakaua Ave.). Recently renovated, the amazing little aquarium harbors more than 300 species of Hawaiian and South Pacific marine life, including the giant clam, the chambered nautilus, and scary sharks. It's the third oldest aquarium in the United States. *Tel. 808/923–9741. Admission: $2.50, children under 15 free. Open daily 9–5.*

㉖ A little farther along Kalakaua Avenue toward Diamond Head is the **Waikiki War Memorial Natatorium.** This open-air structure, which contains the largest swimming pool in the United States, was built to commemorate lives lost in World War II. Although the pool is not recommended for swimming (the eels have made it their home), the beach adjacent to the Natatorium offers some of the best swimming in Waikiki. The memorial, though showing wear and tear, stands proudly and was recently saved from a wrecker's ball. *Admission free. Open 9:30–5.*

Time Out Close by, at the **New Otani Kaimana Beach Hotel** (2863 Kala-
㉗ kaua Ave.), you can dine outdoors beside the sand in the shade of a *hau* tree. This spot is not well known to tourists, but it's one of the nicest oceanfront dining options on the island.

You might be lucky enough to spot *Magnum, P.I.* star Tom Selleck on the sands in front of the **Outrigger Canoe Club,** one of his favorite haunts. The club is private, but not the beach.

28 You could walk over to the **Kapiolani Park Rose Garden** at Paki Street and Monsarrat Avenue, but it's a long walk, and if you come from an area where roses thrive, you've probably seen better. There are picnic tables and the admission is free.

A Waikiki Hike

29 For those willing to do more strenuous walking, the hike to the summit of **Diamond Head** offers a marvelous view. Drive along Diamond Head Road, on the Waikiki side of the extinct volcano. The entrance to the crater is marked by a road sign. Drive through the tunnel to the inside of the crater, once a military fortification.

You can also take a bus from Waikiki. Bus No. 58, "Hawaii Kai-Sea Life Park," stops near the entrance. A sign points the way.

The trail begins at the parking lot. Signs tell you that the hike takes an hour, but you can probably do it in 40 minutes, even with a child in tow. Most guidebooks also say there are 99 steps on the trail to the top. That's true of one flight, but there are four flights altogether. Bring a flashlight to see your way through a narrow tunnel. The view is worth it when you get there, sweeping across Waikiki and Honolulu in one direction and out to Koko Head in the other, with Diamond Head Lighthouse and surfers and Windsurfers scattered like confetti on the cresting waves below. *Park hours daily 6 AM–6 PM.*

You can also walk the 2.3 miles from the zoo to the crater and then climb the additional .7 mile to the 760-foot summit. A group meets Saturdays at 9 AM by the rainbow windsock at the zoo entrance. All but the last part of the hike is escorted and narrated by volunteer guides. Everyone gets a free souvenir "I Climbed Diamond Head" badge. *Tel. 808/944–0804. Donation: $3, free for children.*

A Waikiki Dive

An authentic submarine now operates just off Waikiki. *Atlantis,* which has been taking tourists down to the sea in ships at Caribbean sites for many years, now does Waikiki dives aboard a 65-foot, 80-ton sub carrying up to 40 passengers. Price includes a catamaran ride board the *Hilton Rainbow I* to the dive site and a tour of the Waikiki and Diamond Head shoreline. The sub dives up to 100 feet to see a sunken ship and an artificial reef populated by brilliant fish. While the man-made concrete reef looks more like a fish tenement, it is drawing reef fish back to the area. *Hilton Hawaii Hawaiian Village Pier, tel. 808/522–1710. $67 adults, $33.50 children 4–12. Note: Flash photography will not work. Use film speed 200 or above without flash.*

Beaches

The 2½-mile strand called Waikiki Beach is actually a lei of beaches extending from the Hilton Hawaiian Village on one end to Diamond Head on the other. All of Hawaii's beaches are public, so you can plunk down with aplomb in front of the most elegant hotel.

There are some words of caution to keep in mind when approaching any Hawaiian beach. Take notice of the signs. If they warn of dangerous surf conditions or currents, pay attention. Before you stretch out beneath a swaying palm, check it for coconuts. The trade winds can bring them tumbling down on top of you with enough force to cause serious injury. And don't forget the sunscreen. The sun-protection factor in some new preparations now goes higher than 29. It's a good idea to reapply sunscreen after swimming. Waikiki is only 21 degrees north of the equator, and the ultraviolet rays are much more potent than they are at home. Also, no alcoholic beverages are allowed on the beaches, which is why you may notice some people drinking out of brown paper bags.

30 Waikiki begins at the Hilton Hawaiian Village, where it's called **Kahanamoku Beach and Lagoon.** The swimming is good here, the surf gentle, and the snorkeling not bad. You may find the water in the lagoon a touch too torpid, but it's perfect for small children, and you can lazily paddle around in a little boat. The area is named after Hawaii's famous Olympic swimming champion, Duke Kahanamoku. There's a snack concession, a surfboard- and beach-equipment-rental shop, showers, catamaran cruises, and a volleyball court.

31 Next door is the broad swath of sand at **Fort DeRussy Beach.** The beach is widest here and trails off to a coral bottom in the ocean. There are volleyball courts, cooking stands, picnic tables, dressing rooms and showers, and snack concessions. The beach is frequented by military personnel but open to everyone.

32 Go around the curve to **Gray's Beach** in front of the Halekulani Hotel. A little lodging house, Gray's-by-the-Sea, once was on the Halekulani site and left its name behind. The Hawaiians used to consider this spot a place for spiritual healing and baptism and called it *Kawehewehe*, the removal. The sand here is often covered by high tides. Beyond the reef are two good surfing spots called Paradise and Number Threes. You'll also find food concessions, surfboard- and beach-equipment-rental shops, and canoe and catamaran rides.

Probably the best swimming, and certainly the most activity, is at the part of the beach fronting the Royal Hawaiian Hotel and the Sheraton Moana Surfrider. There are snack bars, catamaran rides, and outrigger canoe rides, and you can sign up for a surfing lesson. The little stretch in front of the Royal Hawaiian is known as **Kahaloa,** while in front of the Sheraton Moana Surfrider it's called **Ulukou.** The Royal Hawaiian cordons off a small section of sand in front, which brings to mind a rich kid's sandbox.

35 The heart of beach activities is next to the Sheraton Moana Surfrider at the **Waikiki Beach Center.** Facilities include public rest rooms, with changing rooms, showers, and a snack stand. The police station is located here.

36 Next you'll come upon **Kuhio Beach Park,** which extends from the Waikiki Beach Center to a wall jutting into the ocean. The wall acts as a breakwater to keep the shoreside waters calm. The area is deceptive, though, and children should be watched closely because there are unpredictably deep holes in spots. (There have been several drownings here.) Beyond the wall, surfers and bodysurfers ride the waves. The wall is a great place for sunset watching, but be careful of your footing.

Beyond the wall, toward Diamond Head, is what is known as the other end of Waikiki. The beaches here laze along the front of Kapiolani Park, beginning with **Queen's Surf Beach.** A curious mixture of families and gays gather here, and it seems like someone always has a bongo drum. There's a lawn and good shade trees. This is a nice place for a sunset picnic.

The Waikiki War Memorial Natatorium punctuates the shoreline with the largest swimming pool in the United States. The pool has no shallow end and depth varies with the tide. The pool isn't very appealing; there are stories of eels in it, which is enough to keep most swimmers away (*see* Tour 3 in Walking Tours of Waikiki, above).

For recommended swimming, go next door to **Sans Souci Beach,** which extends from the Natatorium to the Kaimana Beach Hotel. It's shallow, sandy, and safe for children. The beach is a favorite with singles.

The **beach in front of the exclusive Outrigger Canoe Club** has a good natural sand bottom and is fine for swimming.

What to See and Do with Children

A full moon over Diamond Head, the sound of the surf, the romantic strumming of a ukulele, flower-perfumed air, a gentle breeze—and the kids? Friends may think you've gone over to the far side, but in Waikiki it is possible to have it all—romance and good family fun. Hawaii is a family-centered society, and Waikiki, surprisingly, is a family kind of place. When you need time on your own, many hotels have excellent baby-sitting services and exciting summer and holiday programs to keep your children entertained.

The Hawaiian word for child is *keiki* (CAKE-ee). Many restaurants offer special keiki menus. There are keiki events and keiki admissions to attractions at reduced rates or for free.

The beach is the big draw. With a shallow, sandy bottom, reef-protected waters, and gentle waves, **Waikiki Beach** is safe. There are concessions all along the strand for snacks, and umbrella and raft rental (*see* Beaches, above). You can sign up the children for surfing lessons to learn Hawaii's sport of kings. Catamaran sails take the family to sea for an hour, a half-day snorkel trip, or a sunset cruise. There are outrigger canoe rides and aqua-bikes (*see* Participant Sports in Chapter 6). The best swimming spots for small children are the walled-in area in front of the Holiday Inn and the lagoon at the Hilton Hawaiian Village. There are playground fixtures at **Queen's Surf Beach.** All beaches in Hawaii are open to the public. Be sure to use sunscreen on tender young skin, and reapply often.

Other Waikiki attractions especially for children include:

Honolulu Zoo. There's a petting zoo, an elephant show, a Farm in the Zoo and a tower to climb to look the giraffes right in the eye (*see* Tour 3 in Walking Tours of Waikiki, above).

Zoo Fence Art Mart. On Wednesdays, Saturdays, and Sundays there's usually an artist who will do while-you-wait pastel portraits of children.

Waikiki Aquarium. *2777 Kalakaua Ave. Tel. 808/923–9741. Admission: $2.50 adults 17 and older. Open daily 9–5.*

Kapiolani Park. Adjacent to the zoo, it offers 140 acres in which to run free. There's good family fun at the free Kodak Hula Show, including children's hula lessons (*see* Tour 3 in Walking Tours of Waikiki, above).

Diamond Head Hike. It takes a 6-year-old hiker 40 minutes to get to the top. Bring a flashlight for the tunnel.

U.S. Army Museum at Fort DeRussy This is for young Rambo fans. (*see* Tour 1 in Walking Tours of Waikiki, above).

Pacific Beach Hotel. One thousand fish live in the lobby of this hotel, housed in a 280,000-gallon aquarium (*see* Tour 2 in Walking Tours of Waikiki, above).

Kahala Hilton Hotel. A lagoon with porpoises is the feature. *5000 Kahala Ave., tel. 808/734–2211. Feeding times: 11* AM; *2,* and *4.*

Hilton Hawaiian Village Hotel. The newly landscaped grounds are practically a bird park with macaws, flamingoes, penguins, and more. *2005 Kalia Rd., tel. 808/949–4321.*

Ilikai Waikiki Hotel. A glass elevator whisks you to its top-floor Annabelle's lounge with breathtaking views. Try a frosty virgin chichi for the children. It's coconut and pineapple juice minus the alcohol. The elevator operates from 5 PM. *1777 Ala Moana Blvd., tel. 808/949–3811.*

Beyond Waikiki **Hawaii Children's Museum.** The theme of the museum will be "You the Child," with opportunities to learn about the body, tracing a family tree, and ethnic heritage, plus a Bug Zoo. *Dole Cannery Sq., 650 Iwilei Rd., Honolulu 96817, tel. 808/522–0040. Admission: $5 adults, $3 children 3–8. Closed Mon.*

Hawaii Maritime Center. Many of the center's exhibits are targeted for children. Climb aboard a reproduction of a Matson liner, see a whaling film, explore a real four-masted sailing ship.

Paradise Park. Visitors enter through a huge aviary. The highlight is the performing bird show, 10:25 AM and 1:30 and 3:30 PM. Other attractions: nature walks, "Animal Quackers Review," "Dancing Waters" lighted fountain show, having your picture taken with magnificent macaws (*see* Sights around Honolulu in Chapter 4).

Polynesian Cultural Center. You get around this 40-acre park by tram, canoe, or on foot. Children will have so much fun they won't even notice they're getting an education (*see* Sights around Oahu in Chapter 4).

Sea Life Park (*see* Sights around Oahu in Chapter 4).

Waimea Falls Park. Bring along swimsuits for the children—they'll enjoy a dunk under the falls (*see* Sights around Oahu in Chapter 4).

Restaurants Hawaii has most of the big burger and fried-chicken chains. There are also some unique restaurants offering more than food. The restaurants outlined here are not necessarily recommended for their food, but for some feature that children will enjoy. In all cases, the food is acceptable.

Oceanarium. The restaurant wraps around the huge aquarium and its feeding times are scheduled at the diners' mealtimes (*see* Restaurants in Waikiki in Chapter 7).

Tahitian Lanai. You can reserve your own little thatch dining hut and pretend to be castaways (*see* Restaurants in Waikiki in Chapter 7).

Bobby McGee's Conglomeration. The staff dress in costume: Robin Hood may present the menu and bring the steaks. *2885 Kalakaua Ave., tel. 808/922–1282. Reservations recommended. Dress: aloha. AE, DC, MC, V. Dinner only, Mon.– Thurs. 5:30–10, Fri. and Sat. 5–11, Sun. 5–10. Moderate.*

The Willows. Keikis will like the ponds of prize carp and the thatched-roof pavilions. Famous "sky high" pies for dessert, in flavors like banana or macadamia nut, make this a favorite of small diners (*see* Restaurants near Waikiki in Chapter 7).

Pagoda. Japanese and American cuisine is served in a setting of Japanese gardens, open pavilions, and carp ponds. The carp are fed daily at 8 AM, noon, and 6 PM. *Near Waikiki at 1525 Rycroft St., tel. 808/941–6611. Reservations recommended. Dress: aloha. AE, CB, DC, MC, V. Daily lunch and dinner. Moderate.*

Windows of Hawaii. The views from this revolving restaurant are spectacular, but the food is not exceptional. *1441 Kapiolani Blvd., 23rd floor, tel. 808/941–9138. Reservations recommended. Dress: aloha. AE, CB, DC, MC, V. Daily lunch and dinner. Moderate.*

Makai Market. Located in the Ala Moana Shopping Center, the market offers 20 separate food outlets and one central seating area. The children can have their fries and pizza while you dine on Thai, Japanese, Chinese, or health food, all at bargain prices (*see* Chapter 5).

Food Court. International Market Place. Separate food outlets and one central seating area offer Greek, Japanese, Chinese, Korean, Filipino, and burger and rib fare. *Inexpensive (see* Tour 2 in Walking Tours of Waikiki, above).

Island Treats   **Shave ice.** A local version of the snow cone. Order it with ice cream and skip the azuki beans—children will hate the beans.

Manapua. A rice-flour bun with Chinese-style meat filling is the local equivalent of a hamburger.

Crack Seed. This is the most popular treat with Island children. It is, however, an acquired taste. A good flavor for beginners is wet mango.

Waikiki for Free

Aside from the obvious things like sunshine and sand, there are many attractions and events in Waikiki and around the island of Oahu that are free.

This section includes both attractions that are covered elsewhere in the book and additional attractions that are described here for the first time. They are divided into those that are in Waikiki and those that are beyond Waikiki, and they are listed alphabetically. Also, many hotels provide free hula lessons, lei-making classes, exercise sessions, and other entertainment for their guests. Be sure to check your hotel's activities desk.

In Waikiki   **Chinese cooking class.** Learn to prepare classic Chinese dishes and sample the results at the Great Wok of China restaurant.

*Royal Hawaiian Shopping Center, 2233 Kalakaua Ave., Bldg.
B, 3rd floor, tel. 808/922-5373. Fri. 11:30 AM.*

Damien Museum (*see* Tour 2 in Walking Tours of Waikiki,
above).

Exercise class. Bring a towel or mat for an outdoor session on
the lawn. *Fort De Russy Beach, in front of the Hale Koa Hotel,
2055 Kalia Rd., Mon.–Sat. 9 AM; closed Sun.*

Fashion show. The latest resort fashions are paraded through
the beautiful atrium of the Hyatt Regency Waikiki by Hawaii's
top models. *2424 Kalakaua Ave., tel. 808/923-1234. Wed. 4PM.*

Honolulu marathon clinic. Lectures and instructions on running are given by experts, then participants break into groups,
depending on level of ability and experience, for a run around
the park. *Kapiolani Bandstand, Kapiolani Park, tel. 808/734-
7200. Sun. 7:30 AM.*

Hula lessons. Learn the real hula from a certified hula teacher.
*Royal Hawaiian Shopping Center, 2201 Kalakaua Ave., Bldg.
C, 3rd floor, tel. 808/922-0588. Mon., Wed., and Fri. 10:30 AM.*

Karate. Take a lesson in one of the Asian martial arts. *Waikiki
Community Center, 310 Paokalani Ave., tel. 808/923-1802.
T'ai chi lessons (another martial art) are given Wed. and Fri.
11 AM.*

King's Village (*see* Tour 2 in Walking Tours of Waikiki, above).

Polynesian Cultural Center Mini Show. The enthusiastic young
entertainers from Hawaii's number-one paid visitor attraction
stage a miniproduction. Of course they're hoping you'll rush
right into their Waikiki ticket office and sign up for the complete package, but there's no pressure. *Royal Hawaiian Shopping Center, 2201 Kalakaua Ave., Bldg. C, 1st floor, tel. 808/
922-0588. Tues., Thurs., Sat. 9:30 AM.*

Porpoise Feeding. Kahala Hilton (*see* What to See and Do with
Children, above).

Tennis courts. For public courts in Waikiki, *see* Participant
Sports in Chapter 6.

Wildest Show in Town. The zoo, which normally charges admission, is free after 4 PM. A free show is staged under the big
banyan tree. The bill includes a wide variety of entertainment
from rock to puppet shows. *Honolulu Zoo, 151 Kapahulu Ave.,
tel. 808/971-7171. June, July, and Aug. only, Wed. 6 PM.*

Evening at City Hall. A free concert is offered on the fourth
Thursday of each month in the courtyard of City Hall. *King and
Punchbowl Sts., tel. 808/527-5666. Concerts start at 7 PM.*

Zoo Fence Art Mart (*see* Tour 3 in Walking Tours of Waikiki,
above).

Beyond Waikiki **Aloha Tower** (*see* Sights around Honolulu in Chapter 4).

Arizona **Memorial** (*see* Sights around Oahu in Chapter 4).

East-West Center. Located on the University of Hawaii campus,
the center was founded to promote understanding among the
people of Asia, the Pacific, and the United States. There are
some fascinating buildings and gardens, especially the Japanese garden. The center offers free tours. Reservations are not
required, except for groups. Meet at Jefferson Hall. *1777 East-*

West Rd., tel. 808/944–7691. Bus No. 4 "Nuuanu-Dowsett" from Waikiki. Wed. 1:30 PM.

Humanities Conversation. A lecture and discussion on history, literature, philosophy, or culture is held by the Hawaii Committee for the Humanities. *1802 Keeaumoku St., Honolulu, tel. 808/732–5402. First Wed. of each month, 4 PM. No meetings in January. Shuttle bus No. 17 from Ala Moana Shopping Center.*

Hawaii State Capitol. The architecture of this building, which is surrounded by a moat and held up by volcano-shaped columns, was inspired by Hawaii's unique island geography and geology and by the prevailing spirit of aloha. Legislative sessions are open to the public. Take a free one-hour tour, which includes a visit to the offices of Governor John Waihee and Lieutenant Governor Ben Cayetano. Arrange a tour by stopping in at the Sargeant-at-Arms office, Room 036. You should probably make reservations to ensure that there will be a guide available. *415 S. Beretania St., tel. 808/548–7851. Weekdays 8–5. Bus No. 2 from Waikiki.*

Helemano Plantation. Five acres of flowers, fruits, and vegetables are maintained by disabled citizens working in a vocational training program. It also offers classes in lei making and hula. A gift shop and restaurant are on the site. *64-1510 Kamehameha Hwy., adjacent to the Dole Pineapple Pavilion, tel. 808/622–3929. Daily 7:30–5. Bus No. 8, 19, or 20 from Waikiki to Ala Moana Shopping Center, then transfer to No. 55, "Circle Island," going west.*

Honolulu Academy of Arts (*see* Sights around Honolulu in Chapter 4).

Honolulu Hale. The lovely Spanish Colonial–style building is Honolulu's city hall. There are often art exhibits showing the work of local artists. At Christmas, the lobby is filled with decorated trees and becomes one of Honolulu's prime attractions. A free booklet describing the building is available from the mayor's office on the third floor. *Corner of King and Punchbowl Sts., tel. 808/523–4385. Bus No. 2 from Waikiki.*

Hoomaluhia Botanic Garden Guided Nature Walk. Exotic flora from around the world are growing in this 400-acre garden. Bring light rain gear, insect repellent, and lunch. Reservations are necessary. *End of Luluku Rd., Kaneohe, tel. 808/235–6636. Sat. 10 AM for a 3.4-mi walk; Sun. 12:30 PM for a 2-mi walk. Bus No. 55 "Kaneohe" from Ala Moana Shopping Center.*

Iolani Palace grounds. The Royal Hawaiian Band holds a free concert every Friday from 12:15 to 1. Pick up a picnic lunch, sit on the lawn, and enjoy the music. This series is popular with the downtown office workers. *King and Richards Sts., tel. 808/527–5666.*

Kaneaki Heiau. An impressive ancient Hawaiian temple has been partially restored and includes a prayer tower and several thatched buildings on massive stone platforms. It is located beyond the Sheraton Makaha Resort. *Phone Sheraton's guest services desk, tel. 808/695–9511, to be sure it's open before the long ride out. 84-626 Makaha Valley Rd. Tues.–Sun. 10–2; closed Mon. Bus No. 51 "Makaha" from Ala Moana Shopping Center.*

Kawaiahao Church (*see* Sights around Honolulu in Chapter 4).

Keaiwa Heiau State Park. This temple of the old religion of Hawaii was used as a place of healing. Labeled medicinal plants are maintained by the state parks division. The park also contains the Aiea Loop Trail, an easy 4.8-mile mountain hike. Look for the remains of a Japanese plane that crashed into the mountain during the attack on Pearl Harbor. *Aiea Heights Dr., tel. 808/548–3179. Open 7–4. Bus No. 11 "Aiea Heights" from Ala Moana Shopping Center.*

Koko Head Arboretum Gardens (*see* Scenic Drives around Oahu in Chapter 4).

Lyon Arboretum. Affiliated with the University of Hawaii, this 200-acre garden is tucked in lush Manoa valley, adjacent to the popular (and paying) tourist attraction, Paradise Park. It features a wide variety of tropical flora. *3860 Manoa Rd., tel. 808/ 988–3177. Open weekdays 9–3, Sat. 9–12; closed Sun. Free guided tours first Fri. and third Wed. at 1 PM, third Sat. at 10 AM. Bus No. 5 from Ala Moana Shopping Center to the end of the line, a 45-min ride.*

Mayor's Aloha Friday Music Break. Downtown office workers gather around the fountains at lunch to enjoy a concert. The entertainment is varied and may be anything from a school choir to one of the big-name Hawaii groups. There are several fast-food restaurants bordering the square, so you can pick up a picnic. *Tamarind Park, corner of Bishop and King Sts., tel. 808/ 527–5666. Fri. only, noon. Bus No. 2 from Waikiki.*

Royal Mausoleum. Six of Hawaii's eight monarchs are buried in this 3-acre plot: Kings Kamehameha II, III, IV, V, Kalakaua, and Queen Liliuokalani. *2261 Nuuanu Ave., Honolulu. Weekdays 8–4. Bus No. 4 "Nuuanu" from Waikiki.*

Tennent Art Foundation Gallery. The works of celebrated Island artist Madge Tennent are displayed here. Her subjects are Polynesian and her interpretations are massive in stature, conveying both power and a sensuous softness. *203 Prospect St., tel. 808/531–1987. Tues.–Sat. 10–2; Sun. 2–4. Bus No. 15 from the main depot.*

Young People's Hula Show. The Kapiolani Butterworth children's hula group presents the songs and dances of various Pacific islands. The young dance students are delightful. *Ala Moana Shopping Center, Ala Moana Blvd. and Atkinson Dr., tel. 808/946–2811. Sun. 9:30 AM. Bus No. 8, 19, or 20 from Waikiki.*

4 Excursions from Waikiki

Sights around Honolulu

Numbers in the margin correspond with points of interest on the Downtown Honolulu map.

---

❶ Bishop Museum and Planetarium

Anyone who is interested in any facet of Hawaiian or Pacific culture should make this stop. Artifacts from the centuries before Western contact are included, as well as monarchy-era treasures. There are lustrous feather capes; scary god images; the skeleton of a giant sperm whale; an authentic, well-preserved grass house; and changing displays of old photographs and ethnic crafts. The planetarium next door spotlights "Eyes of Hawaii," a lectured show. *1525 Bernice St., tel. 808/ 847–3511. Admission: $4.95, including the planetarium. Open daily 9–5; closed Christmas.*

Getting There   **By Car:** Lunalilo Freeway to Houghtailing Street exit. Make an immediate right onto Houghtailing Street and then a left onto Bernice Street.

By Bus: No. 2—"School Street"—from Waikiki. Get off at the Kam Shopping Center, walk makai (toward the ocean, south) one block to Bernice Street, and go left.

Escorted Tours   *See* Guided Tours in Chapter 1.

❷ Chinatown

The old section of downtown Honolulu is crammed with interesting shops. Slightly on the tawdry side, it has lately been getting a piecemeal face-lift as little art galleries take up residence in renovated structures. There are lei stands, herb shops, acupuncture places, noodle factories, Chinese restaurants, and a colorful Asian-style open market. Bakeries sell dim sum, sweet rice cakes, Chinese cookies, and sugared ginger. Wo Fat (115 N. Hotel St., tel. 808/537–6260) is a good, popular restaurant, but almost any little restaurant will have authentic food. If you're pressed for time, the most interesting street is Maunakea Street, between Hotel and King streets. Chinatown is on the National Register of Historic Places. *Bordered by River St., Nuuanu Ave., Beretania St., and Nimitz Hwy.*

Getting There   **By Car:** Nimitz Highway to Bethel Street

By Bus: No. 2 from Waikiki.

Escorted Tours   Chinese Chamber of Commerce offers tours every Tuesday 9:30–12:30. The tour includes the Kwan Yin Temple adjacent to the Foster Botanic Gardens. *42 N. King St., tel. 808/533–3181. Cost: $4; add $5 if you want lunch.*

❸ The Contemporary Museum

This exciting new art museum with seven galleries focuses on art of the last four decades by both Hawaiian and Mainland artists. One gallery has a 25-foot ceiling and a bridge for viewing exhibits from above. *2411 Makiki Heights Dr., Honolulu, tel. 808/526–1322. Admission: $3 adults, $1 children 6–14. Open Mon.–Sat. 10–4, Sun. noon–4; closed Tuesday.*

Getting There **By Car:** Ala Wai to Kalakaua Avenue. Right on Kalakaua to King Street. Right on King Street one block to Punahou Street. Left on Punahou Street to Nehoa Street. Left on Nehoa Street two blocks to Makiki Street. Right on Makiki Street one block to the fork. Go left at the fork on Makiki Heights Drive for ⅔ mile.

By Bus: No. 15 from Waikiki.

---

❹ Dole Cannery Square

A cannery was never so glamorous. The Dole pineapple people spent $3.3 million on the tour facility at the 60-year-old pineapple processing factory. Tours start with a fast-paced, 10-minute multi-image stereo slide show telling you everything you ever wanted to know about pineapple. The tour of the canning facility is 40 minutes and ends in the bright Dole Cannery Square, a complex of shops and a cafeteria with a 250-seat atrium. Yes, there is a free tasting room. A new children's museum is open at the square. There is a separate admission charge of $5 for adults, and $3 for children 4–18. *650 Iwilei Rd., tel. 808/ 531–8855. Cost: $5 for the tour and slide show. Access to the square, restaurant, and shops is free. Open 9–5. Tours every 15 min., last tour 3 PM.*

Getting There **By Car:** Nimitz Highway to Summer Street, left on Iwilei Road.

By Bus: No. 8–"Airport/Hickam"—from Waikiki or the Dole Pineapple Transit, departing Waikiki every 10 minutes. Cost: 50¢. Tel. 808/543–6500.

Downtown Honolulu

Hawaii's royal past is set like a jewel in a modern city studded with palms. Office workers wear colorful muumuus and aloha shirts. The Fort Street Mall, closed to traffic, is a hub of lunchtime activity, with shoppers, street preachers, an occasional musician, and people snacking at outdoor tables and benches.

Getting There **By Car:** Ala Moana to Nimitz Highway. Turn mauka (toward the mountains, north) on Alakea Street. There's a municipal parking lot, often full, on Hotel Street between Alakea and Richards streets, with entrances on both Alakea and Richards streets. Private lots are expensive. Metered parking is often available along King Street by Iolani Palace, but be sure to move your car before 3:30 or it will be towed away—no maybes.

By Bus: No. 2 from Waikiki. Get off at Alapai Street and walk makai (toward the sea, south) toward King Street. Most of the historic sites are clustered within easy walking distance.

Escorted Tours "Historic Downtown Walking Tour," tel. 808/531–0481. Cost: $7. Weekdays 9:30 AM. Volunteers from Mission Houses Museum lead this two-hour trek.

Main Points of Interest

❺ **Mission Houses Museum.** The historic complex was home to the first American missionaries in Hawaii. Arriving in 1820, the stalwart band gained royal favor and influenced every aspect of island life. Their descendants have become leaders in government and business and still shape Hawaiian life. The white

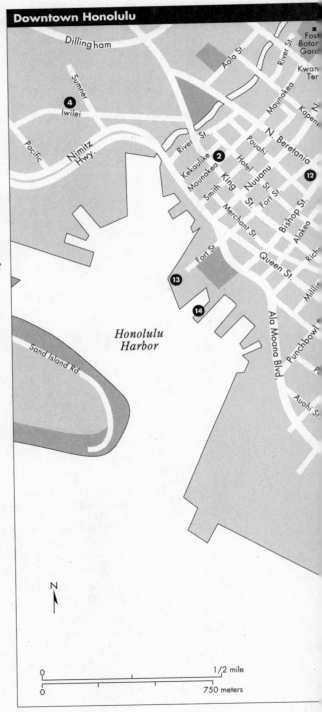

Downtown Honolulu

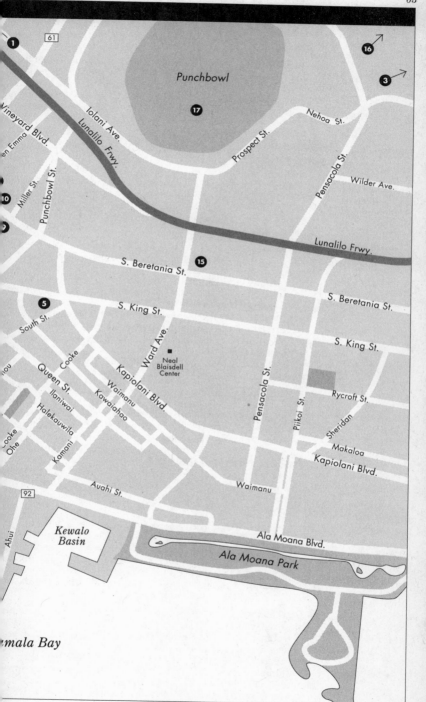

Punchbowl

17

16

3

1

61

Vineyard Blvd.

en Emma Blvd.

Iolani Ave.

Lunalilo Frwy.

Nehoa St.

Prospect St.

Pensacola St.

Wilder Ave.

Miller St.

Punchbowl St.

10

9

Lunalilo Frwy.

S. Beretania St.

15

S. Beretania St.

S. King St.

S. King St.

5

South St.

Cooke

Ward Ave.

Neal
Blaisdell
Center

Kapiolani Blvd.

Pensacola St.

Piikoi St.

Rycroft St.

iou

Queen St.

Iliniwai

Waimanu

Kawaiahao

Sheridan

Makaloa

Halekauwila

Kapiolani Blvd.

Cooke

Ohe

Kamani

Waimanu

Auahi St.

92

Kewalo
Basin

Ahui

Ala Moana Blvd.

Ala Moana Park

mala Bay

frame house was prefabricated in New England and shipped around the Horn. *553 S. King St., tel. 808/531–0481. Admission: $3.50 adults, $1 children. Guided tour included. Open daily 9–4.*

❻ Kawaiahao Church. Fancifully called Hawaii's Westminster Abbey, the coral-block church has witnessed the coronations, weddings, and funerals of a procession of Hawaiian royalty. Graves of missionaries and King Lunalilo are in the yard. The upper gallery has an exhibit of paintings of the royal families. Sunday services are in English and Hawaiian, 10:30 AM. Visitors are welcome and are often offered a tour of the church. *King St. and Punchbowl St., tel. 808/522–1333.*

❼ Kamehameha I Statue. The gilt-robed statue of the Big Isle chieftain, who united all the warring Hawaiian Islands into one kingdom, stands with outstretched arm in welcome. The original is in Kapaau near the birthplace of the king. In back of the statue is Aliiolani Hale, the old judiciary building that once served as the Parliament during the monarchy era. *King St. between Punchbowl St. and Mililani St.*

❽ Iolani Palace. The graceful Victorian structure was built by King David Kalakaua on the site of an earlier palace. Beautifully restored, it is America's only royal palace, containing the thrones of King Kalakaua and his successor (and sister) Queen Liliuokalani. Also on the palace grounds is the Kalakaua Coronation Bandstand, where the Royal Hawaiian Band plays at noon most Fridays. Office workers stand for Hawaii's anthem, *Hawaii Ponoi.* Also see Iolani Barracks, built to house the Royal Guard, and the huge old banyan tree in the back. *King St. at Mililani St., tel. 808/522–0832. Admission: $4, $1 children under 12; children under 5 are not permitted. Open only for guided tours, Wed.–Sat., 9–2:15. Reservations advised.*

❾ Hawaii State Capitol. Built in 1969, this architectural gem is richly symbolic. Columns look like palm trees, legislative chambers are shaped like volcanic cinder cones, and the central court is open to the sky, symbolizing Hawaii's open society. It is surrounded by reflecting pools, as the Islands are surrounded by water. Between the capitol and the palace is a statue of Queen Liliuokalani, Hawaii's last reigning monarch. Out in front is a statue of Father Damien, the Belgian priest who gave his life laboring among the victims of Hansen's disease, or leprosy, on the island of Molokai. *Beretania St. between Punchbowl St. and Richards St.*

❿ Washington Place. The gubernatorial mansion is home to Governor John Waihee, the first Hawaiian to head the ship of state since the overthrow of the monarchy. Queen Liliuokalani lived in the graceful 1846 mansion until her death in 1917. You can only peer through the wrought iron gates, since the residence is not open to the public. *320 S. Beretania St., almost across the street from the Hawaii State Capitol.*

⓫ Two historic churches are in the downtown area. **Saint Andrew's Cathedral,** Episcopal headquarters in Hawaii, is at Beretania and Queen Emma streets, next to Washington Place. Queen Emma, widow of Kamehameha IV, supervised the construction of the church and was baptized in the sanctuary. The building was designed in England, and parts of it were shipped from there. **⓬** **Our Lady of Peace Cathedral** is the main cathedral for the Roman Catholic Church in the Hawaiian Islands. It was built in 1840 after edicts against Catholicism were abolished. It is an unimposing but pretty building, at the head of the Fort Street Mall, near Beretania Street.

⑬ Aloha Tower. When it was built in 1921, it was the tallest building in Honolulu. The 10th-floor observation deck offers 360-degree views of the city and the harbor. This is where visiting ocean liners tie up, including the interisland cruise ships, the SS *Independence* and the SS *Constitution*. *At the foot of the Fort St. Mall, on the waterfront. Admission free. Open daily 8AM–9 PM.*

⑭ Kalakaua Boat House. This newly opened maritime center at Pier 7, near the Aloha Tower, features lively exhibits on everything remotely related to the sea, including marine medicine, whaling, seaplanes, and the latest maritime technology. There are Polynesian voyaging canoes, and you can step aboard a re-creation of a Matson luxury liner. Moored outside is the four-masted square-rigger *Falls of Clyde*, the only one of its kind surviving. It has been faithfully restored as a museum ship. Close by is the *Hokule'a*, the Polynesian sailing canoe that made history. Built according to ancient specifications, the canoe, in a two-year voyage, traced the epic explorations by the Polynesians in the Pacific. The museum's restaurant, Coasters, is one of Honolulu's few waterfront dining spots (see Restaurants near Waikiki in Chapter 7).

---

⑮ Honolulu Academy of Arts

A happy mixture of East and West characterizes the 37 galleries that open into one another and six courtyards. Paul Gauguin's work resides with 13th-century Japanese scrolls. Lunch is served by volunteers in the pretty **Garden Cafe** (tel. 808/531–8865), Sept.–May, Tues.–Fri., 11:30 and 1. Dinner Thurs., 6:30. Reservations are necessary. The Academy Gift Shop is well stocked with books and ethnic crafts. *900 S. Beretania St., tel. 808/538–1006. Admission free. Open Tues.–Sat. 10–4:30, Sun. 1–5. Free guided tours Tues., Wed., Fri., and Sat. 11 AM; Thurs. 2 PM; Sun. 1 PM.*

Getting There By Car: Use the Honolulu city map. The Academy is on the corner of Ward Avenue and Beretania Street. Ample metered street parking is in the area.

By Bus: No. 2 from Waikiki.

---

⑯ Paradise Park

A colorful tropical rain forest is home to macaws and cockatoos that perform on the high wire and do other circus-act tricks. The more than 100 species of plants are labeled, and there's a "dancing waters" fountain show. This is a good photography stop, especially if you're not the outdoors type who gets into the "real" country. *3737 Manoa Rd., tel. 808/988–6686. Cost: $7.50 adults, $6.50 children 13–17, $3.75 children 4–12. Open 10–5. Closed Christmas Day.*

Getting There By Car: Use the Honolulu city map. Go mauka (toward the mountains, north) on University Avenue, staying on it when it becomes Oahu Avenue. Follow Oahu Avenue to the end, then bear right onto Manoa Road.

By Bus: Tel. 808/988–2141 for hours and stops on the park's free shuttle service. Also take No. 8, 19, or 20 from Waikiki to Ala Moana Shopping Center, then transfer to No. 5 to the end of the line, a 45-minute ride.

⑰ Punchbowl National Memorial Cemetery of the Pacific

The names that the ancient Hawaiians gave to places have proven to be strangely prophetic. Puowaina, which means "Hill of Sacrifice," is the name of the extinct volcano whose crater serves as the final resting place of America's heroes. The imposing marble slabs of the "Courts of the Missing" list the names of 26,280 men and women missing in wars. Among the famous entombed here are World War II correspondent Ernie Pyle and Hawaii's astronaut Ellison Onizuka, who died in the *Challenger* space shuttle disaster in 1986.

There are panoramic views of the island from the crater rim. *2177 Puowaina Dr., tel. 808/541–1430. Admission free. Open in winter daily 8–5:30, in summer 8–6:30.*

Getting There **By Car:** You'll need a Honolulu city map. Enter by Puowaina Drive.

By Bus: Take No. 2 from Waikiki to downtown Honolulu, then transfer to No. 15. The bus lets you off on Puowaina Drive for a half-mile walk to the crater. Tell the driver where you're going when you board.

Escorted Tours Punchbowl is included in most city tours (*see* Guided Tours in Chapter 1).

Sights around Oahu

Numbers in the margin correspond with points of interest on the Oahu map.

❶ Arizona Memorial

The *Arizona* Memorial is America's memory book of the attack on Pearl Harbor that plunged the nation into the war in the Pacific. The gleaming white memorial shields the hulk of the USS *Arizona*, which sank with 1,102 men aboard and burned for two days. The names of the men are engraved on a wall of white marble. The ship's flag is mounted on one of the few parts of the *Arizona* still above water.

A free shuttle boat operated by the National Park Service takes visitors to the memorial. You assemble at the Visitor Center, where you'll be assigned to a group. While waiting for your group to be called, you may visit the museum, with its historical photographs and newspaper accounts of the attack, as well as a scale model of the *Arizona*.

Before boarding the shuttle boat, you will be shown a 20-minute documentary of the attack on Pearl Harbor. The boat ride takes you through the part of the harbor that suffered the heaviest bombing. In all, the United States lost 18 ships and more than 3,000 men.

For safety reasons, no children under 45 inches tall are permitted aboard the shuttle or the memorial. Also prohibited are people in bathing suits or with bare feet.

After visiting the memorial, you may tour the USS *Bowfin*, a World War II submarine, moored near the Visitor Center. You will be issued a "wand" for a self-guided tour that takes you through seven (out of eight) of the vessel's compartments, including the torpedo room and engine room. *USS* Arizona *Memorial and Visitor Center. U.S. Naval Reservation, Pearl Harbor, tel. 808/422–0561. Admission free. Tues. is the most crowded, with afternoon waits sometimes as long as 2 hours. Late in the week and early in the day are your best bets. Open Tues.–Sun. 8–3.*

Getting There   **By Car:** Kamehameha Highway. Go past the main Nimitz Gate to Pearl Harbor and watch for the Halawa Gate and the *"Arizona* Memorial" sign. You will be making a left turn coming from Waikiki. Allow 30 minutes.

By Bus: Take No. 20 from Waikiki. You can also take the *Arizona* Memorial Shuttle Bus (tel. 808/946–4747), which is direct. Cost: $2.

Escorted Tours   Cruises to Pearl Harbor leave Fisherman's Wharf twice daily at 9:30 AM and 1:30 PM and last about three hours. They are narrated water tours along the coastline with snacks included. None is permitted to land at the *Arizona* Memorial, as the free park service tour does. Cost about $15. **Power boats: Hawaiian Cruises,** tel. 808/947–9971; **First Pearl Harbor Cruise,** tel. 808/ 536–3641; **Sailboats: Aikane Catamarans,** tel. 808/522–1533.

❷ Byodo-In Temple

Dramatically set against the sheer green cliffs of the Koolau Mountains, this temple is a replica of a 900-year-old temple in Kyoto, Japan. It is surrounded by Japanese gardens and a 2-acre lake stocked with prize carp. A two-ton statue of Buddha presides over all. *47–200 Kahekili Hwy., Kaneoha, tel. 808/ 239–8811. Admission: $1.50 adults, $1 senior citizens, 75¢ children under 12. Open daily 8–4:30.*

Getting There   **By Car:** Likelike Highway to Kahekili Highway. Turn mauka (toward the mountains, north) at the Valley of the Temples Memorial Park and drive through the cemetery area.

By Bus: No. 8, 19, or 20 from Waikiki to Ala Moana Shopping Center, then transfer to No. 55—"Kaneohe–Kahaluu." Ride to the Temple Valley Shopping Center (an hour ride). The Byodo-In Temple is about a mile hike from here.

❸ Polynesian Cultural Center

This is Hawaii's number one paid visitor attraction. Situated on Oahu's North Shore, it consists of 40 acres of lagoons and seven South Pacific "villages" representing Hawaii, Tahiti, Samoa, Fiji, the Marquesas, Aotearoa (New Zealand), and Tonga. Travel about by foot, tram, or canoe. There are colorful pageants, shows, and food and craft demonstrations throughout the day. Run by the Mormon Church, it provides the opportunity for Pacific Islanders to earn tuition and passage to attend the adjacent Brigham Young University's Hawaii cam-

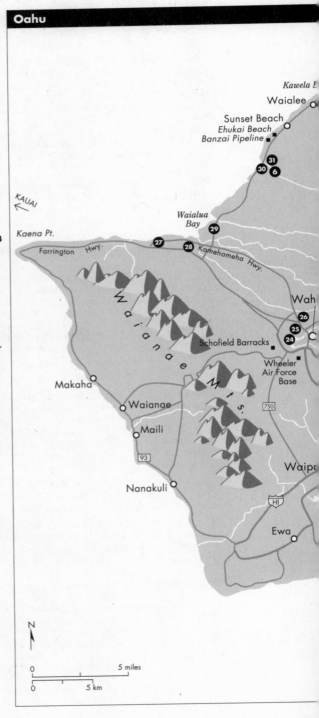

Oahu

pus. There's a dinner buffet and a spectacular evening show. There is also a PCC luau that features an imu ceremony with lots of pageantry and a buffet of Hawaiian food and familiar favorites, including a salad bar. The emphasis is more on fun than on authenticity. It is timed so that you can attend the luau at 6 PM and go to the big show afterward. It's worth a day's outing by itself. If you're short of time, you can try to sandwich it in on a driving tour of the island, knowing you'll miss much of what makes this attraction so popular. The center's new IMAX theater, scheduled to be open by the time you read this, will seat 600 people. The screen will be 90 feet wide by 65 feet high. The center is producing its own film on Polynesia. *55–370 Kamehameha Hwy., Laie, tel. 808/293–3333, or in Waikiki 808/923–1861 or 800/367–7060. Cost (general admission to all villages and daytime shows): $25 adults, $10 children 5–11. Complete package (includes general admission, all afternoon shows, dinner, and the evening show): $39 adults, $20 children 5–11. Ambassador Passport (this is the VIP ticket that includes everything in the other two passports, plus kukui nut lei greeting, an escorted tour, choice of buffet dinner or luau and special seating at the evening show): $70 adults, $45 children 5–11. Admission, Luau, Show Package : $45 adults, $26 children 5–11. Open Mon.–Sat. 12:30–9 PM. Closed Thanksgiving and Christmas.*

Getting There   **By Car:** Kamehameha Highway. Allow about 1½ hours from Waikiki.

By Bus: No. 8, 19, or 20 from Waikiki to Ala Moana Shopping Center, then transfer to No. 55—"Circle Island"—going west to Polynesian Cultural Center.

Escorted Tours   *See* Guided Tours in Chapter 1.

❹ Sea Life Park

The park enjoys one of the most beautiful settings on the island at Makapuu Point, guarded by a lighthouse and studded with offshore islands. There are performing porpoise, penguin shows, a whale show spiced with local legend and history, sea lions, and turtles. The big feature is the 300,000-gallon Hawaiian Reef Tank, a real reef enclosed in glass and circled by a spiral walkway that descends 3 fathoms deep. Visible are sharks, moray eels, manta rays, and schools of jewel-toned tropical fish. The nautical Galley restaurant gets an A on view and "passing" on food. The whaling museum, with its scrimshaw exhibits, is small but well done. *Makapuu Point, Waimanalo, tel. 808/259–7933. Admission: $9.95 adults, $7.75 juniors 7–12, $3.75 children 4–6. Open Sun.–Thurs., and Sat 9:30–5—last show at 4:30; Fri. 9:30–10 PM—last show at 7:45 A Hawaiian show starts at 8:30 PM.*

Getting There   **By Car:** Kalanianaole Highway. Allow 40 minutes from Waikiki.

By Bus: No. 58—"Hawaii Kai–Sea Life Park"—from Waikiki Stand on ocean side of Kuhio Avenue to catch the bus.

❺ Senator Hiram Fong's Plantation

Hiram Fong served as Hawaii's senior U.S. Senator for 1 years. Now he and his family have opened their 725-acre plan tation in lush Kahaluu for tours. A tram takes visitors t sections of the garden named for the U.S. presidents under whom Fong served. President Kennedy Valley has mango, lychee, and sugarcane among its flora while President Ford Plateau has a northwest-American theme. *47–285 Pulama Rd., Kahaluu, tel. 808/239–6775. Cost: $6.50 adults, $3 children 5–12. Open daily 9–4. 45-min tram tours leave every 20 min.*

Getting There **By Car:** Kamehameha Highway. Allow 40 minutes from Waikiki.

By Bus: No. 8, 19, or 20 from Waikiki to Ala Moana Shopping Center, then transfer to No. 55.

❻ Waimea Falls Park

Nestled in historic Waimea Valley on Oahu's North Shore, the park contains remnants of the early Hawaiian civilization. The garden trails are well marked and the plants are labeled. More than 2,500 species of flora from all over the world, many endangered, are the pride of the park. Stroll about or take the narrated tram ride included with the admission charge. There's swimming at the 45-foot falls. Hawaiian games and dances are presented, along with cliff diving. There's a restaurant and picnic areas. Twice a month at the full moon, the park is open for free "moonwalks." *59–864 Kamehameha Hwy., Haleiwa, tel. 808/638–8511. Cost: $9.95 adults, $6 children 7–12, $2 children 4–6. Moonwalks are free. Open daily 10–5:30.*

Getting There **By Car:** Kamehameha Highway, opposite Waimea Bay. Allow one hour from Waikiki.

By Bus: No. 8, 19, or 20 from Waikiki to Ala Moana Shopping Center, then transfer to No. 52 or 55.

Scenic Drives around Oahu

The eastern end of Oahu is suburbia, trailing off into the bush and to stretches of golden beach. The bays of the windward coast possess, or are possessed by, magnificent mountains that reach down almost to the shore in places. Yet, thanks to two tunnels through the mountains, Honolulu commuters bed down here in natural splendor after a day of work. The wild North Shore is a surfer's paradise, wild and windswept in winter, placid as an old retriever in summer. The leeward side, close to town, is a jumble of developments housing the burgeoning population of Honolulu, but the farther you go, the sunnier, the drier, and the more Hawaiian it gets before the road ends and Oahu's essentially untamed nature asserts itself. The central plains have plantations that grow pineapple and sugarcane.

A few advisories: Some beaches are extremely dangerous, especially in the winter months, and few are manned by lifeguards. If you see a sign warning of dangerous surf or currents, pay attention. Don't walk out on rocky promontories for a better view. A sudden set of huge waves can sweep you out to sea. If you go hiking, don't go alone. You don't know the territory, and some valleys are subject to flash floods after heavy rains. Should you encounter trouble, and you can, there won't be any help around. Hawaii's wilderness is accessible to all types, so never leave valuables in your car. Criminals can spot a rented car a mile away; even if they're caught, they count on the fact that the visitor will be long gone before the case comes to trial.

For this guide, the island is divided into two car trips, the Eastern Ring and the Pearl Harbor–North Shore Circuit. You can skip the dry leeward coast unless you're going to play golf at the Sheraton Makaha. If you are pressed for time, combine the Eastern Ring with the North Shore Circuit (reading the North Shore text backward) and do it in a day, carefully budgeting your time. Be sure to get a road map. Your car-rental agency will provide an adequate one.

Those of you who want to make these trips on a guided tour should review the Guided Tours section of Chapter 1. The Circle Island and Half-Circle tours are the most popular offerings, and cover most of the highlights.

It is also possible to circle the island by bus, taking either No. 57 or No. 58 from the Ala Moana Shopping Center to tour the East Oahu Ring and No. 52 or 55 to tour the North Shore Circuit. Ask your driver about transfer points.

Whether you're driving, taking a tour, or riding the bus, reading this section will give you an idea of what you want to see. Ready? For mood music as you go, KCCN 1400 on your AM radio dial plays Hawaiian music exclusively.

Numbers in the margin correspond with points of interest on the Oahu map.

The East Oahu Ring

❼ Drive toward **Diamond Head.** The extinct volcanic landmark is really named Leahi. It got its common name when some sailors thought they had found precious gems on the slope. The diamonds proved to be volcanic refuse. The Diamond Head light is the brightest light in the Pacific. Surfers gather at the two scenic pullouts.

Where Diamond Head Road becomes Kahala Avenue, you'll find yourself in Oahu's wealthiest neighborhood, where the oceanfront homes have been sold for more than $20 million, mostly to Japanese investors.

At periodic intervals along the tree-lined street are narrow lanes that provide access to the beach for the public. The swimming is best at Hunakai Street. There's also Kahala Beach Park with showers and picnic tables under the trees, just before the Waialae Country Club.

❽ Kahala Avenue ends at the **Kahala Hilton Hotel** (500 Kahala Ave., tel. 808/734–2211), with its gardens and porpoise pond. Feeding times are 11 AM, 2 PM, and 4 PM.

From Kahala Avenue, take a mauka turn (toward the mountains, north) on Kealaolu Avenue, skirting the private **Waialae Golf Course,** scene of the annually televised Hawaiian Open tournament. This will take you onto the Lunalilo Freeway, which quickly becomes Kalanianaole Highway.

During rush hour, this road is a traffic-choked commuter corridor all the way to the sprawling Hawaii Kai residential development. The valley once flourished with ancient Hawaiian fish ponds. Now the waterways are lined with suburban homes with two cars in the garage and a boat out back. There's a pullout overlooking Hawaii Kai and its shopping malls. The late Henry J. Kaiser was the developer.

❾ The first real stop is **Hanauma Bay.** Turn makai (toward the ocean) at the sign. Even from the overlook, the horseshoe-shaped bay is a beauty with its coral reefs clearly visible through the turquoise waters (*see* Participant Sports in Chapter 6). A little jitney will run you down the steep slope to the beach, which was the setting for the film *From Here to Eternity.*

The drive along the **Koko Head** shoreline—untamed and open to the ocean—is a big favorite on the island. Offshore, the islands of Molokai and Lanai call like distant sirens, and every once in a while, Maui is visible in blue silhouette. You can stop **❿** at every scenic pullout. One has the famous **Halona Blowhole,** a lava tube that sucks in the ocean and then spits it out in lofty plumes. The spot is frequented by petty thieves, so lock up when you get out to look.

⓫ The long stretch of inviting beach you'll see is **Sandy Beach.** Tempting as it looks, it is not advisable to swim there. Notice that the only people in the water are local and young. They know the powerful and tricky waves well. Even so, many of them end up in the hospital every year. Back and neck injuries are common here due to powerful shore breaks.

Beyond Sandy Beach is the area known as **Queen's Beach.** This whole shoreline is currently the center of a fight between developers and conservationists. Conservationists won the last round on Election Day, but the battle's not over yet.

The **Koko Head Arboretum Gardens,** which is on the mauka side (toward the mountains, north) of the highway at Kealahou Street, will appeal to you if you like cacti.

Get ready for one of the most beautiful vistas in the world. Just past the **Hawaii Kai Championship Golf Course,** the terrain **⓬** gets even drier and the road climbs toward **Makapuu Point.** As you round the bend, the beauty of the windward side bursts on you—mountains and bay, ocean and islands. It's exhilarating.

The Makapuu Lighthouse is nestled in the cliff face. The two offshore islands are the large **Rabbit Island** and the smaller **Turtle Island.** The distinctive peninsula in the distance is **Mokapu,** site of a U.S. Marine base. The spired peak in the mountains is Mount Olomana. The long pier in front of you is part of the Makai Undersea Test Range, a research facility that does not permit visitors. The facility recently launched a manned submersible to study Loihi, the active undersea volcano that is forming another Hawaiian island. In about a thousand years, Loihi should surface.

The beautiful cove at Makapuu is great for seasoned bodysurfers, but it can be treacherous. There are fine, safe beaches farther along, so save your swimming.

Colorful hang gliders often soar in the breezes, leaping from those imposing cliffs. It takes a lot of daring. There have been several fatalities here, as you can imagine.

The marine attraction, **Sea Life Park,** is definitely worth a stop. In its finned menagerie, it has the world's only "wholpin," offspring of a romance between a whale and a dolphin. Even if you've been to other marine parks with their trained cetaceans, you may like the distinctive Hawaiian flavor that permeates this one (*see* Sights around Oahu, above).

Past Sea Life Park, the beaches are safe for swimming. **(13) Waimanalo Beach Park** often draws young toughs with a chip on their collective shoulder. Pass it by.

Time Out On the mauka side (toward the mountains, north) of the road, just opposite Bellows Air Force Base, there's usually a little gathering of crafts people who sell everything from homemade goodies to shell jewelry. Also in this area is the best Mexican restaurant on the island, **Bueno Nalo** (41–865 Kalanianaole Hwy., tel. 808/259–7186; no reservations and, with luck, no line), and **Harry's**—an unpretentious bakery with delicious cinnamon rolls.

A right turn just after the McDonald's brings you to **Sherwood Forest,** a public beach open on the weekdays. It's a good **(14)** bodysurfing beach. Just past Sherwood Forest is **Bellows Beach,** open to the public on weekends. The beach is uncrowded and great for both swimming and bodysurfing. There's plenty of shade here, too.

(15) The town of **Waimanalo** has traditionally been a depressed area. Down the side roads, going toward the mountains, are little farms that grow a variety of fruits and flowers. There's a **Dave's Ice Cream** here with flavors like lychee and mango. Dave's has some of the best ice cream in the Islands.

If you see any trucks selling corn on the cob and if you're in a condominium where you can cook it, be sure to get some. It may be the sweetest you'll ever eat.

(16) If you want to take a detour to **Kailua Beach,** which many people consider the best on the island, turn right at the big Castle Hospital junction of Kalanianaole Highway and Kailua Road. Keep going straight, no matter how many times the road changes its name, until it forms a T with Kalaheo Avenue. Make another right on Kalaheo until you come to the corner of Kailua Road. On one side is the **Kalapawai Market.** Generations of children have gotten their beach snacks here. Across the street is the **Kailua Beach Center,** where you can rent windsurfing equipment and arrange for lessons at either Naish Hawaii or Kailua Sailboards. **Wild Bill's Sandwich Saloon** will fix you up with a lunch, and you can find the latest in bikini fashions at Naish Hawaii.

If you go makai (toward the ocean, south) by the market, you'll be right at Kailua Beach. There are showers and picnic areas.

If you are not going to continue around the island, you can stay here knowing you can be back in Waikiki in about 40 minutes. The only time constraint will be if you want to visit the Queen Emma Summer Palace (read on), which closes at 4 PM.

Retracing your route to the main junction, the sights include **(17) Ulu Po Heiau,** which will look like a pile of rocks to the uninitiated. Ulu Po Heiau is a temple platform that dates back to ancient times. It's behind the YMCA (1200 Kailua Rd.).

The swath of green meadow is Kawainui Marsh, which overflowed on New Year's Eve, 1987, causing parts of Kailua to be declared a disaster area. Mud three to five feet thick was deposited in homes.

(18) Instead of turning at the junction, continue straight toward the mountain, up and through the Pali Tunnel. Watch for the turn-off to the **Pali Lookout** (Nuuanu Pali). Mark Twain called the view from here the most beautiful in the world.

King Kamehameha I fought the decisive battle for control of Oahu here, driving the defending forces over the edge of the 1,000-foot cliffs.

As you drive back toward Honolulu, the road will be lined with sweet ginger during the summer. If it has been raining, water-falls will be tumbling down the sheer green cliffs of the Koolaus.

(19) On the left is the **Queen Emma Summer Palace.** The white mansion, which once served as the summer retreat of King Kamehameha IV and his wife, Queen Emma, is now a museum maintained by the Daughters of Hawaii. It contains many excellent examples of koa furniture of the period, including the beautiful cradle of Prince Albert, heir to the throne, who died at age 4. *2913 Pali Hwy., tel. 808/595–3167. Admission: $4. Open weekdays 9–4; Sat. 9–noon; guided tour, Mon. 2 PM.*

There's one more scenic pullout on the way to downtown Honolulu. It overlooks a pagoda, which makes a lovely silhouette against a setting sun.

Stay right on the Pali Highway and it will go straight into Bishop Street through downtown Honolulu. A left turn on Ala Moana Boulevard will lead you into Kalakaua Avenue in Waikiki.

North Shore Circuit, Including Pearl Harbor

There are two alternate routes to get to the Lunalilo Freeway from Waikiki. On the Diamond Head end, go mauka (toward the mountains, north) on Kapahulu Avenue and follow the signs leading you to the freeway. On the ewa end (away from Diamond Head, west), take Ala Wai Boulevard and turn mauka at Kalakaua Avenue, staying on that until it ends at Beretania Street, which is one way going left. Turn right at Piikoi Street, and the signs will direct you onto the freeway heading west.

(20) The freeway will merge with Moanalua Freeway, Route 78. Stay with this past **Moanalua Gardens,** a lovely park with huge spreading monkeypod trees. A hula festival is held on the ancient hula mound every July (tel. 808/839–5334 for information on the Prince Lot Hula Festival and escorted hikes into historic Moanalua Valley).

(21) You'll also pass **Aloha Stadium,** where the seating configuration changes at the touch of a switch to conform to the type of event, whether football, baseball, or rock concert.

(22) As you approach the stadium on the freeway, bear right at the sign to Aiea, then merge left onto Kamehameha Highway Route 90, going south to **Pearl Harbor.** Turn right at the Halawa Gate (*see* Sights around Oahu, above, for details on visiting Pearl Harbor).

After Pearl Harbor, retrace your steps and take either Kamehameha Highway or H–2 Freeway to Wahiawa, home of the U.S. Army base at Schofield Barracks. You'll be traveling through pineapple and sugarcane fields to this old plantation town that now has a distinctly military flavor. Segments of *From Here to Eternity* were filmed here.

Time Out A pleasant lunch stop, right on the main road, is **Kemoo Farms** (tel. 808/621–8481). It's a real country restaurant on the shores of Lake Wilson. Lunch is served daily from 11:30 AM to 2:30 PM.

㉓ **The Wahiawa Botanical Gardens**—nice, but not the best in the Islands—are at 1396 California Avenue, tel. 808/621–7321. Open daily 9–4.

From Wahiawa, take Kamehameha Highway, now Route 80. If ㉔ you're interested in seeing the **Hawaiian Birth Stones,** once a sacred site for royal births, take the dirt road on the left, just over the bridge. It's a short ride to the stones.

Back on the main road, you'll come to a scrubby-looking patch ㉕ ambitiously called the **Del Monte Pineapple Variety Garden.** Unpromising as it looks, it's actually quite interesting, with varieties of the ubiquitous fruit ranging from thumb-sized pink ones to big golden ones.

㉖ Just a little farther along is the **Dole Pineapple Pavilion** (64-1550 Kamehameha Hwy., tel. 808/621–8408; open daily 9–5:30). Dole used to give away the juice, but now sells it, and the juice is canned. You can buy chunks of fresh fruit for car snacks. Try a piece of what you buy while you're still in the shop to make sure the pineapple is fresh.

You'll have to make some choices when you come to the traffic circle.

㉗ If you go to **Mokuleia,** you'll come to the polo fields where matches are held every Sunday, March–August, and to the Dillingham Airstrip, where you can watch the gliders or book a sailplane ride with **Hawaii Soaring Club** (tel. 808/677–3404). No reservations, with 20-minute flights every 20 minutes. Cost: $35 for one passenger, $50 for two.

㉘ If you follow the sign to **Waialua,** you'll come across a sleepy old plantation town. There are marked side roads to Haleiwa.

㉙ Another alternative is to head directly to **Haleiwa** (pronounced HAH-lay Eva), a plantation town that's come of age. It used to be a fashionable retreat at the end of a railroad line that no longer exists. During the '60s, the hippies gathered here. Today, both the grand old hotels and most of the hippies are gone. There are still plantation (general) stores, along with beach boutiques and art galleries. Haleiwa is where it's "happening" if you're a young surfer, or if you wish you were. What really puts the town on the map, however, are its two "shave ice" stores, the famous **Matsumoto's** and the number-two-but-trying-harder **Aoki's.** The latter is our favorite. Shave ice is the Hawaiian version of the snow cone. If you want to do it right, get it with vanilla ice cream and azuki beans.

Time Out **Jameson's by the Sea** (62-540 Kamehameha Hwy., tel. 808/637–4336) is a popular restaurant in Haleiwa. Although the road is between the restaurant and the sea, the views are special, especially sunsets from the porch. Another good local restaurant, on the same highway, is **Steamer's** (Haleiwa Shopping Plaza, tel. 808/637–5071), one of those cool, dark, reliable surf-and-turf dining spots.

Leaving Haleiwa and continuing along Kamehameha Highway, you'll pass the famous **North Shore beaches,** where the winter surf comes in monstrous rollers.

30 **Waimea Bay** is a popular family picnic spot. On the mauka side (toward the mountains) of the road is **Waimea Falls Park** (*see* Sights around Oahu, above). There's a restaurant here, and if the surf is up and dangerous, you can swim at the falls in the park.

31 To see a fine example of an ancient temple, take the Pupukea Road mauka (toward the mountains). It's a steep climb, not quite a mile, to the road leading to the **Puu-o-Mahuka Heiau.** This ancient site of human sacrifice is on the National Register of Historic Places. The views are spectacular.

Back down on the coastal road are the famous surfing beaches, **Banzai Pipeline, Ehukai,** and **Sunset,** where the winter surf sometimes crests at 20 to 30 feet. Don't even get close to the water when surf conditions are like that. Leave the sea to the daredevil young surfers.

32 The only hotel of any consequence in these parts is the **Turtle Bay Hilton** (57–091 Kamehameha Hwy., tel. 808/293–8811). You can watch the surf safely from the dining room.

33 The Old Kahuku Sugar Mill on Kamehameha Highway, which shut down in 1971 and enjoyed a brief stint as a tourist attraction, has reopened as **The Mill at Kahuku** (tel. 808/293–2414) with a restaurant and businesses. Visitors may take a self-guided tour of parts of the turn-of-the century mill with its steam engines and enormous gears (admission free; open 10–6). There's also a gift shop and a craft area, but this is rather "run of the mill." The Country Kitchen restaurant, integrated in the mill works, serves an inexpensive menu of burgers, steaks, and sandwiches. It's open for breakfast, lunch, and dinner.

34 Dominating the town of Laie is the Church of Jesus Christ of Latter Day Saints (Mormon). The white **Mormon Temple** (55-415 Iosepa St., tel. 808/293–9167), made of pulverized volcanic rock and coral, was dedicated in 1919. The church operates Brigham Young University's Hawaii campus and the sprawling **Polynesian Cultural Center.** A visit to the center isn't cheap, but it's worth it (*see* Sights around Oahu, above).

35 About 4 miles down the highway, look for the Hawaii Visitors Bureau sign for **Sacred Falls.** It's a wild state park with a strenuous 2-mile hike to an 80-foot waterfall. This is Hawaiian country as you dreamed it would be. Swim in the pool beneath the falls—a happy alternative to the commercial Waimea Falls Park. Don't attempt the trail if there has been rain; the valley is subject to flash flooding and the trail can be slippery.

At the village of Punaluu, the well-known restaurant **Pat's at Punaluu** (53–567 Kamehameha Hwy., tel. 808/293–8502) sits at the water's edge. After leaving Punaluu, you'll come upon a **36** very pretty cove, **Kahana Bay.** The water is too shallow to enjoy a swim, but it's a lovely, shady spot for a picnic.

Next to the **Kahana Bay Beach Park** is an ancient Hawaiian fish pond that was in use until the 1920s. The Hawaiians were not only expert fishermen, they had learned to raise fish to assure themselves of an ample supply regardless of natural conditions. Modern researchers have only recently reinvented the fish farm.

The next thing to look for, although it's not spectacular, is the **Crouching Lion** mountain formation. It's on the ridge line behind an inn of the same name. As you continue driving along the shoreline, you'll notice a picturesque little island called, for obvious reasons, **Chinaman's Hat.**

At the town of Waiahole is a little market with the unlikely name, Hygienic Store. Here you can branch off to Kahekili Highway (Rte. 83) and head for the Valley of the Temples and its lovely **Byodo-In Temple** (*see* Sights around Oahu, above). It's a chance to be still and to contemplate all that has unfolded in your day's tour.

Continue on Kahekili Highway to the Likelike Highway (Rte. 63), where you turn mauka (toward the mountains) and head back toward Honolulu through the Wilson Tunnel. The highway leads to the Lunalilo Freeway going east. Exit at Pali Highway and go south through downtown Honolulu to Nimitz Highway, then turn left on Ala Moana Boulevard, which leads to Kalakaua Avenue.

5 Shopping

Introduction

Islanders used to wait until they traveled to shop because there wasn't much here. Now the treasures of the world have come to this Pacific crossroads. The merchandise is the latest, and the prices are competitive.

The Hawaiian fashion industry is the state's third largest business, behind tourism and agriculture. Muumuus (the lovely, flowing, loose-fitting garment worn by Hawaiian women) and aloha shirts (sport shirts in tropical prints) are worn in the office and at parties. Almost every visitor buys at least one Hawaiian garment. Getting into costume is part of the fun of any Hawaiian vacation.

Hawaii is also one of the leaders in the manufacture of resort wear. Many shops carry seasonal clothing, woolens, and leathers, catering to the needs of visitors who might not have the leisure to shop at home. There's even a fur salon, **Jindo,** at the Hyatt Regency Waikiki (2424 Kalakaua Ave.).

Beyond fashion, many gift items are unique to Hawaii. The cultural diversity of the Islands and the state's ties to Asia are reflected in a cornucopia of unusual shops.

The following credit card abbreviations are used: MC, Master-Card; V, Visa.

Aloha Shirts and Muumuus For stylish Hawaiian wear, the kind worn by local men and women, look in **Liberty House** at 2314 Kalakaua Avenue, and other locations throughout the Islands; **Carol & Mary,** at the Halekulani and Hilton Hawaiian Village hotels; and **Andrade,** at the Royal Hawaiian and King's Village shopping centers as well as at the Hyatt Regency Waikiki, Princess Kaiulani, Royal Hawaiian, Sheraton Moana Surfrider, and Sheraton Waikiki hotels. If you want something bright, bold, and cheap, there are any number of "garment factory to you" outlets and street stalls. Don't bother with free buses that offer to take you to a factory. They're a waste of limited vacation time and the factory bargains aren't exceptional.

Oldie aloha shirts have become collectibles. Discerning buyer and owner of **Paradise Antiques** (3rd floor, Royal Hawaiian Shopping Center, 2233 Kalakaua Ave., tel 808/922–5615), Colleen Nicol, has assembled quite a selection, ranging in price from $55 for a 1950s manufactured shirt to $1,000 for an authentic 1930–1940 aloha shirt. Years before she opened her shop, Nicol also was an avid collector of costume jewelry and has a dazzling display of great rhinestone stuff.

Just beyond Waikiki, **Bailey's Antique Clothing and Thrift Shop** (758 Kapahulu Ave.) also carries vintage aloha shirts along with furniture and old wicker.

High Fashion **Liberty House** is again recommended. **Carol & Mary** has been known for high quality and designer labels since 1937. **Altillo** (2117 Kuhio Ave. and a new location in Kahala Mall) carries a line of European menswear, with shirts ranging from $20 to over $200. **Chocolates for Breakfast,** in the Waikiki Shopping Plaza, is the trendy end of the high fashion scene. For the latest in shoes and bags, **C. June Shoes,** in the Waikiki Trade Center, displays an elegant array of unusual and *expensive* styles. **Mosaic,** on the 10th floor of the Waikiki Business Plaza, just across

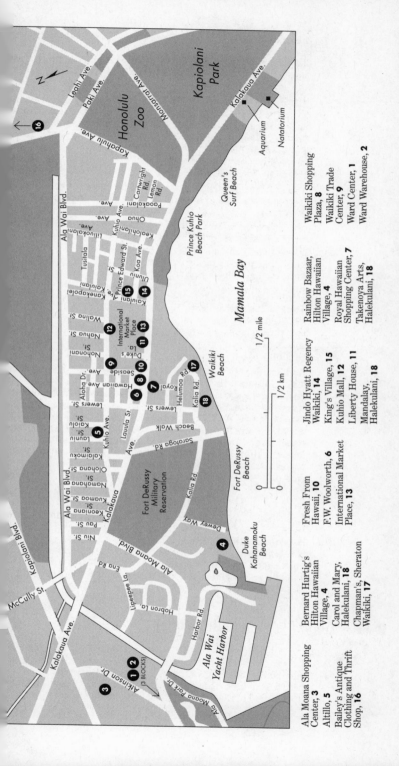

Ala Moana Shopping
Center, **3**

Altillo, **5**

Bailey's Antique
Clothing and Thrift
Shop, **16**

Bernard Hurtig's
Hilton Hawaiian
Village, **4**

Carol and Mary,
Halekulani, **18**

Chapman's, Sheraton
Waikiki, **17**

Fresh From
Hawaii, **10**

F.W. Woolworth, **6**

International Market
Place, **13**

Jindo Hyatt Regency
Waikiki, **14**

King's Village, **15**

Kuhio Mall, **12**

Liberty House, **11**

Mandalay,
Halekulani, **18**

Rainbow Bazaar,
Hilton Hawaiian
Village, **4**

Royal Hawaiian
Shopping Center, **7**

Takenoya Arts,
Halekulani, **18**

Waikiki Shopping
Plaza, **8**

Waikiki Trade
Center, **9**

Ward Center, **1**

Ward Warehouse, **2**

the street from the Waikiki Shopping Plaza, is a wholesale outlet open to the public. It carries the Mosaic line along with a few other "name" labels. On the same floor, **Leathers of the Sea** has the best prices on eel-skin purses, wallets, and attaché cases.

Resort Wear Clothing **Liberty House** has the widest selection. **Chapman's** at the Sheraton Waikiki, Hyatt Regency Waikiki, Royal Hawaiian, Sheraton Moana Surfrider, Ikikai Waikiki, and Hilton Hawaiian Village hotels and other island locations, is a fine men's specialty shop. **McInerny** has a couple of theme shops and a clearance shop in the Royal Hawaiian Shopping Center. **Andrade** has a compact but good inventory of both men's and women's resort fashions in its hotel shops.

Mature women who like clothing that is conservative and well-designed absolutely rave about **Alfred Shaheen** fashions. See for yourself. They're at the Royal Hawaiian Shopping Center, Rainbow Bazaar, King's Village, Hyatt Regency Waikiki, Ilikai Waikiki, and Sheraton Waikiki.

Food Take home fresh pineapple, papaya, or coconut. Jam comes in flavors like poha, passion fruit, and guava. Kona coffee has an international following. There are lines of dried food products such as *saimin* (Japanese noodle soup), *haupia* (a firm coconut pudding), and teriyaki barbecue sauce. All kinds of cookies are available, as well as exotic teas, drink mixes, and pancake syrups. And don't forget the macadamia nuts. By law, all fresh-fruit products must be inspected by the Department of Agriculture. The following stores carry only inspected fruit, ready for shipment:

The best place to shop for all these delicacies is the second floor of **F. W. Woolworth** (2225 Kalakaua Ave., tel. 808/923–2331). It accepts credit-card (MC, V) telephone orders and ships directly to your home. So do **ABC stores,** with 24 locations in Waikiki (tel. 808/538–6743; MC, V). An outfit called **Fresh From Hawaii** (2270 Kalakaua Ave., Suite 1514, tel. 808/922–5077) specializes in inspected, packed pineapple and papaya, plus gift packs of jams and Kona coffee. It will deliver to your hotel and to the airport baggage check-in counter or ship to the mainland United States and Canada. It also has concessions inside Woolworth's, at the Royal Hawaiian Shopping Center, International Market Place, Outrigger Waikiki Hotel, and Outrigger Reef Hotel; telephone credit-card orders are also accepted (MC, V).

Gifts **Mandalay,** in the Halekulani Hotel (2199 Kalia Rd.), goes in for the ethnic look with lots of Thai imports, caftans, kimonos, exclusive men's shirts, and Issey Miyake designs. Also at the Halekulani, **Takenoya Arts** specializes in intricately carved netsuke (small Japanese ornaments), both antique and contemporary, and one-of-a-kind ivory necklaces, some reasonably priced.

Hawaiian Arts and Crafts One of the nicest gifts is something handcrafted of native Hawaiian wood. Some species of trees grow only in Hawaii. Koa and milo each have a beautiful color and grain. The great koa forests are disappearing because of environmental factors, so the wood is becoming valuable. There are also framed arrangements of delicate *limu* (seaweed), feather leis and polished kukui nut leis, wooden bowls, and hula implements.

The best selection and best prices are at the **Little Hawaiian Craft Shop** in the Royal Hawaiian Shopping Center. The manager is a former librarian and enjoys talking about the ancient arts. Some items are Bishop Museum reproductions, with a portion of the profits going to the museum. The shop also has a good selection of Niihau shell leis (those superexpensive leis from Niihau Island), feather hatbands, and South Pacific arts. Both traditional Hawaiian and more contemporary arts and crafts are featured at the **Kuhio Mall Craft Court.** It's upstairs and hard to find but worth the search. Usually you'll find several artists at work. Prices are reasonable.

Jewelry You can buy gold chains by the inch on the street corner, and jade and coral trinkets by the dozen. **Bernard Hurtig**'s has a fine jewelry department, specializing in 18K gold and antique jade. Hurtig's boutique jewelry is a collection of fabulous fakes, many of them reproductions of famous pieces and priced from $35. Hurtig's is a recognized authority on *netsuke*, the small Japanese sword ornaments carved in jade, ivory, and other precious materials. Waikiki shops are at the Kahala Hilton Hotel (5000 Kahala Ave.) and Hilton Hawaiian Village (2005 Kalia Rd.). **Haimoff & Haimoff Creations in Gold,** located in the Halekulani Hotel (2199 Kalia Rd.), features the original work of award-winning jewelry designer Harry Haimoff.

Tiffany's of Fifth Avenue fame has just opened in the Sheraton Moana Surfrider. It has transported its lovely window designs to this Pacific outpost. Some items are surprisingly inexpensive—and you do get a Tiffany box with your purchase.

Shopping Malls Some Americans still aren't used to the multistory shopping complex, so they don't often stray to the upper levels, where the rents are cheaper and the shops usually are smaller and more original. Waikiki has three such tiered malls, plus several other interesting shopping areas.

The Royal Hawaiian Shopping Center (2201 Kalakaua Ave.), fronting the Royal Hawaiian and Sheraton Waikiki hotels, is three blocks long, containing 150 stores on three levels. There are Paris shops with names like **Chanel, Gianni Versace, Louis Vuitton, Hermès,** and **Cartier** and a shop, **Loewe,** specializing in high-quality leather goods from Madrid. In addition to the **Little Hawaiian Craft Shop** mentioned before, several other stores may be recommended. **Thai Treasures** is a showcase of lovely objects from Thailand, ranging from painted paper and bamboo umbrellas to bejeweled Buddhas. **Boutique Marlo**'s specialty is hand-painted women's clothing, reasonably priced, considering the quality. **The Accessory Tree** carries an assortment of belts, bags, and jewelry, some crafted in shells, others hand-painted, plus a limited but good selection of clothing. **The Swimsuit Warehouse** sells only swimsuits, all at the same price: $20.95.

Time Out Reliable stops for hungry shoppers: the **Great Wok of China,** and the sushi bar at **Restaurant Suntory.** On the light side, try **Island Snow**'s local specialty, "shave ice," a snow cone in flavors like banana, guava, and *lilikoi* (passion fruit). There's also **Baskin Robbins** and **McDonald's.**

The **Waikiki Shopping Plaza** (2270 Kalakaua Ave.) is across the street with its 75-foot-high water-sculpture gizmo (when it's working). Three fashion shops worth looking at are the aforementioned trendy **Chocolates for Breakfast;** its sister store, **Villa Roma,** equally trendy but younger and less expensive; and **Ninalee Boutique** with good-quality linen dresses and well-tailored women's business clothes. There's a **Waldenbooks** with stacks of Hawaiian titles, and a hula show at 6:30 and 8 PM, free with a proof of purchase from a plaza store.

Time Out If it's lunchtime, you're in the right place. **Lau Yee Chai** is a local favorite and the choice of visiting Chinese dignitaries. There's also **Ray's Seafood** and **Tanaka of Tokyo.** A best bet: **Seigetsu** for an inexpensive Tokyo-style *udon* (noodle soup) with tempura.

The Waikiki Trade Center is slightly out of the action (at the corner of Kuhio and Seaside Aves.). The second-floor shops never made it and are now shuttered, but there are some prizes on the ground floor. The **Ruby Begonia** has neon art, lots of gizmos, greeting cards, and wacky souvenirs. **Bebe's Boutique** leans to the leather look; it's for the slim and affluent. **Hawaiian Cotton,** next door, carries attractive sweatpants and tops, and T-shirts. **C. June Shoes,** mentioned earlier, is here.

Time Out The Waikiki Trade Center has one of the best lunch (and dinner) stops in the area, the **Baci** restaurant. The savory Italian entrées include a splendid lobster ravioli.

There are three theme-park-style shopping centers. Right in the heart of Waikiki is the **International Market Place** (2330 Kalakaua Ave.), a tangle of souvenir stalls under a giant banyan tree. They've added a new international **Food Court.** The Market Place spills into adjacent **Kuhio Mall** (2301 Kuhio Ave.), with more of the same beads, beach towels, and shirts. Upstairs at Kuhio Mall is a working gallery called **The Craft Court.** All wares are Hawaiian-made, many right on the spot. They range from pottery to hand-painted shirts and traditional weavings. **King's Village** (131 Kaiulani Ave., across from the Princess Kaiulani Hotel) looks like a Hollywood stage set for old, monarchy-era Honolulu, complete with a changing-of-the-guard ceremony every evening about 6:15. King's Village is good for browsing. **Kitamura's,** way up at the top end of the lane, has a fascinating collection of wooden-faced Japanese dolls, second-hand kimonos from Kyoto that make great jackets, and elaborate formal kimonos. The beautiful obi sashes sold here make lovely table runners. It's hard to leave this store without buying something. Dolls start under $30 and go to the hundreds.

The Rainbow Bazaar at the **Hilton Hawaiian Village** (2005 Kalia Rd.) actually has three themes: Imperial Japan, complete with a Japanese farmhouse; Hong Kong Alley, with a moon gate; and South Pacific.

Even though it is not in Waikiki, the gigantic **Ala Moana Shopping Center** (1450 Ala Moana Blvd.) shouldn't be missed by any serious shopper. It's five minutes from Waikiki on the No. 8 bus; the center is on the corner of Atkinson and Ala Moana boulevards. All the main Hawaiian department stores are here, including **Sears, J.C. Penney,** and **Liberty House.** Stores open their doors weekdays and Saturday at 9:30 AM, Sunday at 10 AM. The shopping center closes weekdays at 9 PM; Saturday it closes at 5:30, and Sunday it closes at 5.

Shirokiya, a Japanese department store, is definitely worth a visit. Someone is usually demonstrating the latest state-of-the-art kitchen gadget in at least two languages, one of them Japanese. The upper-level food section is like a three-ring circus of free samples, hawkers, and strange Japanese specialties, both fresh and tinned. The toy department whirls and clinks with windup wonders.

Time Out People are always lined up for the fast food at **Patti's Chinese Kitchen. The Makai Market** is a food bazaar with 20 independent kitchens serving everything from pizza to health food, poi, ribs, sushi, and Thai food. There's a central seating area, so everyone in the family can try different foods yet dine together.

Farther down Ala Moana Boulevard is the **Ward Center** (1200 Ala Moana Blvd.) and the **Ward Warehouse** (1050 Ala Moana Blvd.). Both are eclectic mixes of boutiques and restaurants, with the Ward Center being a bit more "upscale."

Flea Market The **Aloha Flea Market** at **Aloha Stadium** has great bargains in aloha wear, costume jewelry, and designer fakes plus lots of Asian imports. *Open Wed., Sat., Sun., 6 AM–3 PM. Admission: 35¢. For the Flea Market shuttle bus, call 808/955–4050 for closest pickup point to your Waikiki hotel. Hours: 7:30 AM–10:55 PM. Cost: $6 round-trip, including admission.*

6 Sports

The party is over early in Hawaii because everyone wants to be up, active, and outdoors the next day. Many sporting options are available right in Waikiki, others are close by, and nothing's more than an hour away.

Participant Sports

Biking The good news is that the coastal roads are flat and well-paved. On the down side, they're also awash in vehicular traffic. Frankly, biking is no fun in either Waikiki or Honolulu. Things are a bit better outside the city. Be sure to take along a nylon shell jacket for the frequent showers on the windward side and remember that Hawaii is Paradise After the Fall. Lock your bike or be prepared to hike.

Bicycles are available for rent at **Aloha Funway Rentals** (1984 Kalakaua Ave., tel. 808/947–4579). Day rate: $10 for a six-speed and $13 for an eight-speed. You can buy a bike, or, if you've brought your own, you can get it repaired at **The Bike Shop** (1149 S. King St., Honolulu, tel. 808/531–7071). If you want to find some biking buddies, write ahead to the **Hawaii Bicycling League,** Box 4403, Honolulu 96813, or call 808/988–7175.

Golf The island of Oahu is waffled with golf holes. It has more golf than any other Hawaiian island, and most of the 26 courses are open to the public. A few, such as the Waialae, site of the Hawaiian Open, are private clubs. The closest municipal facility is the **Ala Wai Golf Course** (404 Kapahulu Ave., tel. 808/296–4653) on Waikiki's mountain end, across the Ala Wai Canal. It's par 71 on 6,281 yards and has a pro shop and a restaurant. Greens fees: $18 weekdays; $20 weekends. Rental carts: $11; rental clubs: $10. The waiting list is long, so if you plan to play, call the minute you land. Call at 6:30 AM at least one week in advance.

You'll stand a better chance at the 6,350-yard **Hawaii Kai Championship Course** or the neighboring 2,545-yard **Hawaii Kai Executive Course.** Fees are $50 with a cart for the championship course; and for the shorter Executive Course, $11 weekdays, plus $17.50 for a cart. (Tel. 808/395–2358 for either.) Another good buy: **Olomana Golf Links** on the windward side (41–1801 Kalanianaole Hwy., tel. 808/259–9971). Fees are $39 weekdays and $49 weekends and holidays. **Sheraton** has a course at Makaha (tel. 808/695–9544). Rates: $90 for guests of any Sheraton hotel and $100 for nonguests. The golf course at the **Turtle Bay Hilton** (tel. 808/293–8811), on the North Shore, costs $80 weekdays, $90 weekends.

Horseback Riding There's no riding right in Waikiki and with insurance rates skyrocketing many ranches have closed their operations. **Kualoa Ranch** (tel. 808/237–8515), on the windward side, across from Kualoa Beach Park, still has trail rides in Kaawa, one of the most beautiful valleys in all Hawaii. It also has an activities club; for $90 for the day, you can go horseback riding, try windsurfing, ride a Jet Ski, fly in a helicopter, try a dune buggy, go snorkeling or diving, and have lunch. The ranch will even pick you up in Waikiki for an extra $5. The **Sheraton Makaha** (tel. 808/695–9544) offers one-hour guided trail rides daily except Mondays. Rates: $16 for guests of the Sheraton and $18.50 for nonguests. The **Turtle Bay Hilton** (tel. 808/293–8811) has daily 45-minute trail rides for a cost of $20 for guests of Turtle Bay and $22 for nonguests. Reservations are required.

Jogging The most popular places are the two parks, Kapiolani and Ala Moana, at either end of Waikiki. You can also run a ring around Diamond Head. The fashionable 4.8-mile route takes you past scenic views, luxurious homes, and herds of other joggers. Every Sunday, March–November, at 7:30 AM, there's a free Marathon Clinic that starts at the Kapiolani Bandstand.

Tennis There are four free public courts at **Kapiolani Tennis Courts** (2748 Kalakaua Ave., tel. 808/923–7927); nine at the **Diamond Head Tennis Center** (3098 Paki Ave., tel. 808/923–7927); and 10 at **Ala Moana Park** (tel. 808/521–7664). Several Waikiki hotels have tennis facilities open to nonguests but guests have first preference. The **Ilikai Waikiki Hotel** (1777 Ala Moana Blvd., tel. 808/949–3811) has seven courts, one night lighted, plus a pro shop, daily tennis clinics, instruction, a ball machine, and a video. It also has special tennis packages, including room and court fees. There's one court at the **Hawaiian Regent** (2552 Kalakaua Ave., tel. 808/922–6611), with lessons and clinics by Peter Burwash International. The two courts at the **Pacific Beach Hotel** (2490 Kalakaua Ave., tel. 808/922–1233) also offer instruction.

Water Sports The seemingly endless ocean options include surfing, windsurfing, snorkeling, swimming, scuba, canoeing, bodysurfing, waterskiing, deep-sea fishing, and sailing. Most of these activities can be arranged through any hotel travel desk, beach concession, or at the **Waikiki Beach Center,** next to the Sheraton Moana Surfrider Hotel.

Deep-Sea Fishing Try **Coreene-C Sport Fishing Charters** (tel. 808/536–7472) or **Island Charters** (tel. 808/536–1555), with more than 20 fishing boats. All are berthed in Honolulu's Kewalo Basin. Plan to spend $80–$85 per person, sharing a boat with others for a full day (7 AM–3:30 PM). Half-day rates $65–$75. Charters run $425–$450 for a full day and about $325 for a half day. All fishing gear is included but not lunch. The captain normally expects to keep the fish. Tipping is customary and $20 to the captain is not excessive, especially if you're going to keep the fish you caught.

Sailing Lessons may be arranged through **Tradewind Charters** (350 Ward Ave., Suite 206, Honolulu 96814, tel. 808/533–0220). Instruction is by American Sailing Association standards. Cost: $33 per hour for the first student and $15 for each additional student up to four. Transportation from Waikiki is available. Tradewinds specializes in intimate sunset sails for a maximum of six people, $59 per person, including hors d'oeuvres, champagne, and other beverages. The same price will buy you a half-day snorkel or scuba sail. Yacht charters can be arranged.

Scuba Diving and Snorkeling **Dan's Dive Shop** (660 Ala Moana Blvd., tel. 808/536–6181) offers a catamaran dive trip for $55, and a four-day dive certification program for $370.

The most famous snorkeling spot in Hawaii is Hanauma Bay, a marine-life sanctuary. The picturesque bay is a volcanic crater whose outer wall fell into the ocean. The bay is best early in the morning before the crowds arrive. **Hanauma Bay Watersports** (tel. 808/395–8947) has a half-day Hanauma Bay excursion for $6. **Steve's Diving Adventure** (tel. 808/947–8900) offers the same for $6. The old reliable firm **South Seas Aquatics** (tel. 808/538–3854) has half-day snorkel tours for $35, which includes refreshments and snacks, and beginning scuba instruction at $65.

If you go snorkeling and you're sun sensitive, wear a T-shirt. Those ultraviolet rays go right through Hawaii's crystal clear waters. Bring along a bag of frozen peas; the fish love them.

Surfing If you'd like to try surfing, ask one of the attendants at the beach activities facility in front of the Royal Hawaiian Hotel or Sheraton Moana Surfrider Hotel. They will rent you a board and give you lessons. They insist they'll have you standing on a board and riding a wave on your first outing.

Windsurfing This sport was born in Hawaii, and Oahu's Kailua Beach is its cradle. World champion Robby Naish and his family build and sell boards, rent equipment, run "windsurfari" tours, and offer instruction. They also have the only commercial accommodations on Kailua Beach: **Naish Hawaii** (160 Kailua Rd., Kailua 96734, tel. 800/262-6068).

Spectator Sports

The University of Hawaii Rainbows take to the football field at **Aloha Stadium** (tel. 808/488-9509) in season. There are often express buses from Kapiolani Park (tel. 808/531-1611 for details). **Neal S. Blaisdell Center** (777 Ward Ave., tel. 808/521-2911) hosts, in season, sumo, boxing, and basketball. Polo season starts March 11 and runs every Sunday until the end of August. Game: 2:20 PM., Dillingham Field, Mokuleia (tel. 808/637-7656). Admission $5, children under 12 free. Food concession available, or pack a tailgate picnic.

7 Dining

Introduction

Hawaiian food has always been regarded as not much more than pig, poi, and pineapple. In the past few years, with an influx of highly trained, talented young chefs from Europe, a definite regional cuisine has emerged. It combines the freshest local ingredients (many of them peculiar to Hawaii or the tropics) with the classic cooking techniques of France and Asia, along with nuances of California. It's called Pacific Rim Cuisine.

Because of the strength of the state's tourism industry, the hotels have been able to attract some of the best culinary talent in the world. Consequently, Honolulu, including Waikiki, is one of the few cities where the best dining in town is in the hotels.

A wide variety of restaurants serve excellent ethnic food, especially Chinese and Japanese. So pervasive is the Eastern influence that even the McDonald's menu is posted in both English and *kanji*, the universal script of the Orient, and McDonald's serves, in addition to its regular fare, *saimin*, a Japanese noodle soup that outranks the hot dog and pizza as the local favorite snack.

The dining adventures that await you are diverse. You may dine with silver and fine linen napkins or from monkeypod dishes, using chopsticks, fork, or fingers. There may be candlelight, moonlight, or neon light.

For snacks and fast food, look for the *manapua* wagons, the food trucks usually parked at the beaches; and *okazu-ya* stores, the local version of a deli, dispensing tempura, sushi, and "plate lunch." A good plate lunch has macaroni salad, "two scoops rice," and an entrée that might be curry stew, kalua pig and cabbage, or sweet-and-sour spareribs.

The most popular Hawaiian seafood:

ahi—yellowfin tuna from Hawaiian waters.
aku—skipjack, bonito tuna.
ama ama—choice, seasonal mullet.
mahimahi—dolphin fish, not to be confused with the mammal porpoise.
ono—large mackerel-type fish, considered to be one of Hawaii's best-tasting fish.
opakapaka—blue snapper.
papio—a young ulua or jack fish.
uku—deep-sea snapper.
ulua—crevalle or jack fish.
weke—goatfish.

Fruits you may encounter or should try to include in a meal:

guava—It's the pink juice on the breakfast buffet. It's high in vitamin C and makes good jams, jellies, and sherbets.
mango—Smooth-skinned and yellowish-red on the outside, this juicy fruit has a yellow pulpy interior with a distinctive, sweet flavor. When cooked, a mango's taste is a cross between an apple and a peach.
papaya—This melonlike fruit is also high in vitamin C. Try it with a squeeze of lemon or lime.
passion fruit (lilikoi)—The tart, seedy yellow fruit makes deli-

cious desserts, jellies, and sherbet. A local favorite juice drink is orange-passion.

pineapple—The Hawaiian version is sweeter than most. Choose the darker yellow spears or the chunks down by the base of the plant.

poha—cape gooseberry. Tasting a bit like honey, it makes a great jam.

More local favorites, and common dining terms, some imported from other cultures:

bento—box lunch.

haupia—a light gelatinlike dessert made from coconut.

kalua pig—pork that has been cooked in the *imu* (underground oven).

kaukau—common Hawaiian word for food.

Kona coffee—coffee grown in the Kona district of the island of Hawaii, prized for its robust flavor.

laulau—steamed bundle of ti leaves containing pork, salted butterfish, and taro tops.

lomilomi salmon—shredded salmon, usually raw, massaged to tenderness and mixed with chopped tomato, onion, and ice.

luau leaves—cooked taro tops with a taste similar to spinach.

mai tai—Hawaiian fruit punch with rum.

ono—delicious (adj.), as in ono kaukau.

poi—Hawaiian staff of life, made from cooked taro roots.

pupu—any hot or cold, usually bite-size, appetizer; often served in a varied assortment.

saimin—noodle soup that might include shrimp, green onion, fish cake, and pork.

sashimi—chilled raw fish, thinly sliced.

sushi—a variety of vinegared rice treats. Even novices enjoy "cone" sushi, a sweeter version wrapped in soy crust.

The most highly recommended restaurants in each price category are indicated by a star ★.

Category	Cost *
Very Expensive	over $35
Expensive	$25–$35
Moderate	$15–$25
Inexpensive	under $15

per person without sales tax (4%), service, or drinks

The following credit card abbreviations are used: AE, American Express; CB, Carte Blanche; DC, Diners Club; MC, MasterCard; and V, Visa.

Few restaurants require jackets. Where the suggested dress is "aloha," it means dress nicely but a jacket isn't necessary. An aloha shirt, of course, is perfect.

Restaurants are open daily unless otherwise noted.

Restaurants in Waikiki

Very Expensive

Continental **Bagwells 2424.** A waterfall cascading over etched glass sets the
★ tone for Bagwells, which was recently redecorated in trendy
mauves with crystal chandeliers and an antique Chinese
screen. The nouvelle Hawaiian dishes are innovative and delicious, such as an appetizer of opakapaka in filo pastry on mango
puree or an entrée of broiled ulua on lilikoi beurre blanc with
pink and green peppercorns. The double chocolate pâté with
warm orange zabaglione is a chocoholic's Waterloo. A choice of
three complete dinners ranges from $52 to $68. The adjacent
Wine Bar lists 400 wine selections. Many special wines are
available by the glass. There is also a grazing menu from
Bagwells. A small portion of the ulua entrée goes for a quarter
of the price of a full portion. *Hyatt Regency Waikiki Hotel, 2424
Kalakaua Ave., tel. 808/923–1234. Reservations required.
Dress: jackets suggested but not required. AE, CB, DC, MC, V.*
Maile. The star attraction is an excellent selection of seafood,
ranging from local fish to Maine lobster. Steaks and cuts of
meat are the pride of the restaurant; they come in several sur-
prising combinations. Rotating table d'hôte menus spotlight
"healthy" gourmet fare, without creams or butters, for $52.
*Kahala Hilton Hotel, 5000 Kahala Ave., tel. 808/734–2211.
Reservations required. Dress: aloha. AE, CB, DC, MC, V.*
★ **Michel's at the Colony Surf.** With mirrors, candlelight, piano
music, crystal, and chandeliers, it's easily the most romantic
restaurant in town, right beside the sea. The service is superb.
Michel's is the only restaurant left in Waikiki doing tableside
cooking. Breakfast is an insider's secret. Try starting a day
here with crepes sautéed with fruit in a suzette sauce. *Colony
Surf Hotel, 2895 Kalakaua Ave., tel. 808/923–6552. Reservations required. Dress: jackets at dinner, casual for breakfast
and lunch. AE, CB, DC, MC, V.*

French **La Mer.** In the exotic, elegant atmosphere of a Mandalay man-
★ sion, you'll be served a unique blend of French and nouvelle Hawaiian cuisine that most chefs consider to be the finest dining
experience in Hawaii. Portions are delicate and beautifully
presented. A favorite appetizer is new potato salad with sour
cream and caviar. A sample entrée is breast of duck with fresh
pears and spiced apples in a light ginger juice. Each evening
there are two complete dinner menus, which run from about
$65 to $120, soup through dessert. *Halekulani Hotel, 2199
Kalia Rd., tel. 808/923–2311. Reservations required. Jackets
required. AE, CB, DC, MC, V.*

Expensive

Bali by the Sea. Don't be fooled by the name. This is not an
Asian ethnic restaurant. Like its island namesake, Bali is
breeze-swept and pretty. The food is internationally acclaimed
and features such entrées as roast duck with papaya puree and
macadamia nut liqueur. Pastry chef Gale O'Malley is the only
American pastry chef to be decorated by the French government. *Hilton Hawaiian Village, 2005 Kalia Rd., tel. 808/949–*

Dining

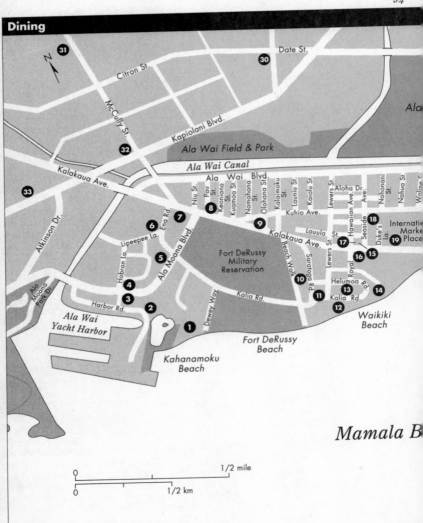

Mamala B

0 ————— 1/2 mile

0 ————— 1/2 km

Alpine Village, **30**

Baci, **18**

Bagwell's 2424, **21**

Bali by the Sea, **1**

Bavarian Beer
Garden, **16**

Beachcomber, **19**

Benihana of Tokyo, **1**

Bon Appetit, **4**

Buzz's Steak and
Lobster House, **10**

Cafe Cambio, **33**

Cafe Regent, **25**

Chart House, **3**

Chez Michel, **6**

Chuck's Steak
House, **11**

Ciao!, **14**

Colony, **21**

Garden Lanai, **26**

Golden Dragon, **1**

Hala Terrace, **29**

Harry's Cafe and
Bar, **21**

Hau Tree Lanai, **27**

Hy's, **23**

Jolly Roger East, **22**

Jolly Roger
Waikiki, **17**

Kacho, **13**

King Tsin
Restaurant, **31**

La Mer, **12**

Lau Yee Chai, **15**

Maile, **29**

Michel's at the Colony
Surf, **28**

Musashi, **21**

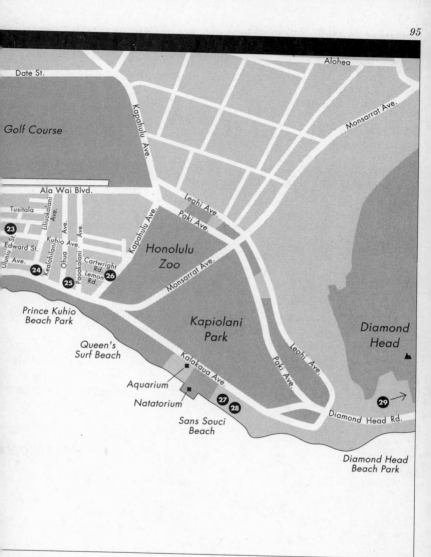

4321. Reservations recommended. Dress: aloha. AE, CB, DC, MC, V.

★ **The Secret.** Formerly known as The Third Floor, it feels like Europe—maybe Spain—with extravagant food displays and big wicker chairs to hide in. You can start with the 20 or so dishes in the appetizer bar and finish with the surprise complimentary dessert, which is wonderful. In between, don't miss the complimentary pâté and the nan bread baked in an earthen oven. *Hawaiian Regent Hotel, 2552 Kalakaua Ave., tel. 808/922–6611. Reservations required. Dress: aloha. AE, CB, DC, MC, V.*

Ship's Tavern. The Moana Hotel's signature dining room uses soft spotlights on each table rather than candlelight. The restaurant features French Continental cuisine with a touch of local nouvelle. It also has an array of fresh seafood specialties. *Sheraton Moana Surfrider Hotel, 2353 Kalakaua Ave., tel. 808/922–3111. Reservations advised. Dress: casual. AE, CB, DC, MC, V.*

French   **Chez Michel.** Tinkling fountains, lattice work, and big wicker chairs are the background for prime French cuisine. If you want to impress someone with an insider's touch of class, this is the spot. *Eaton Square, 444 Hobron La., tel. 808/955–7866. Reservations advised. Dress: aloha. AE, DC, MC, V.*

Japanese   **Kacho.** The city of Kyoto is noted for its fine cuisine, and Kacho
★ is an authentic Kyoto-style restaurant. The tempura teishoku is a complete meal with a good sampling of tastes. The sushi, too, is authentic and fresh. *Waikiki Parc Hotel, 2233 Helumoa Rd., tel. 808/921–7272. Reservations recommended. Dress: aloha. AE, CB, DC, MC, V.*

Seafood   **Nick's Fishmarket.** Television and film star Tom Selleck spent
★ so much time here that he went into partnership with the owners and opened another restaurant, The Black Orchid. His favorite: bouillabaisse. Also recommended: Greek salad and fresh grilled fish of the day. *Waikiki Gateway Hotel, 2070 Kalakaua Ave., tel. 808/955–6333. Reservations required. Dress: aloha. AE, CB, DC, MC, V.*

Steakhouse   **Colony.** Pick your own meat and it's cut to order. This place is known by locals to have consistently fine food. *Hyatt Regency Waikiki, 2424 Kalakaua Ave., tel. 808/923–1234. Reservations required. Dress: aloha. AE, CB, DC, MC, V.*

Moderate

American   **Hala Terrace.** This restaurant has an open-air setting and a healthy lunch menu that stars unusual salads and vegetarian dishes. There is also a full low-calorie menu with calories listed and more traditional offerings, such as a corned beef sandwich on rye with sauerkraut. Dinner starts at 6, and you won't be seated after 7. After that, the Hala Terrace becomes the site on Monday through Saturday of the Danny Kaleikini Show, a delightful Polynesian revue, but the tab is $50 for dinner and show. *Kahala Hilton Hotel, 5000 Kahala Ave., tel. 808/734–2211. Reservations required. Dress: aloha. AE, CB, DC, MC, V.*

★ **Hau Tree Lanai.** A real sleeper, it's often overlooked and shouldn't be. Dine under inviting trees, right beside the sand. The restaurant features Asian and California items, with an emphasis on healthy eating. *New Otani Kaimana Beach Hotel,*

2863 Kalakaua Ave., tel. 808/923-1555. Reservations required. Dress: casual at breakfast and lunch, aloha at dinner. AE, CB, DC, MC, V.

★ **Orchids.** You can't beat the setting, right beside the sea, with Diamond Head looming in the distance and fresh orchids everywhere. It's terraced, so every table has a view. The popovers are huge, and the salads are light and unusual. *Halekulani Hotel, 2199 Kalia Rd., tel. 808/923-2311. Dress: aloha. Reservations recommended. AE, CB, DC, MC, V.*

Plumeria Cafe. This little gem is next to the busy hotel entrance. Featured are seasonal specialties, pasta, salads, and good old-fashioned fountain treats in exotic flavors, such as guava, kiwi, and coconut. *Kahala Hilton Hotel, 5000 Kahala Ave., tel. 808/734-2211. Reservations recommended. Dress: aloha. AE, CB, DC, V.*

Rainbow Lanai. The ocean, waterfalls, and intimacy are the extras. The real treat is the food from the Hilton's award-winning kitchens. *Hilton Hawaiian Village, 2005 Kalia Rd., tel. 808/949-4321. Reservations required. Dress: aloha. AE, CB, DC, MC, V.*

★ **Tahitian Lanai.** Polynesian with a capital P in setting and menu, it's about the only Waikiki restaurant that regularly draws the downtown business crowd at lunch. Try the landmark eggs Benedict. *Waikikian Hotel, 1811 Ala Moana Blvd., tel. 808/946-6541. Reservations required. Dress: casual. AE, CB, DC, MC, V.*

Chinese **Golden Dragon.** Local Chinese people consider this the best.
★ Chef Chang still goes back to China to embellish his skills. He bills his fare as Szechuan, Cantonese, and nouvelle Chinese. Unusual for a Chinese restaurant: desserts other than fortune cookies. *Hilton Hawaiian Village, 2005 Kalia Rd., tel. 808/949-4321. Reservations required. Dress: casual. AE, CB, DC, MC, V.*

French **Bon Appetit.** Excellent French nouvelle cuisine in a cozy atmos-
★ phere is prepared by owner-chef Guy Banal. *Discovery Bay, 1778 Ala Moana Blvd., tel. 808/942-3837. Reservations required. Dress: aloha. AE, CB, DC, MC, V. Closed Sun.*

Italian **Baci.** Nouvelle Italian with such entrées as lobster ravioli. The
★ star appetizer is charcoaled shrimp with lime, mint, and feta cheese. Baci is one of Waikiki's great finds. *Waikiki Trade Center, 2255 Kuhio Ave., tel. 808/924-2533. Reservations recommended. Dress: casual. AE, CB, DC, MC, V.*

Spats. Award-winning cuisine is served in a speakeasy atmosphere. After 8 PM it becomes a popular disco. *Hyatt Regency Waikiki, 2424 Kalakaua Ave., tel. 808/923-1234. Reservations required. Dress: aloha. AE, CB, DC, MC, V.*

Japanese **Benihana of Tokyo.** It's as famous for its theatrical knife work at the *teppan* (iron grill) tables as it is for its food. You will be seated at the same table with other people. *Hilton Hawaiian Village, 2005 Kalia Rd., tel. 808/955-5955. Reservations required. Dress: casual. AE, CB, DC, MC, V.*

Seafood **The Chart House.** Overlooking the Ala Wai Yacht Harbor and the sunset, it's a popular cocktail spot. Dinner specialties are Hawaiian lobster and other seafood. *Ilikai Waikiki Hotel, Marina Bldg., 1765 Ala Moana Blvd., tel. 808/941-6669. Reservations recommended. Dress: casual. AE, CB, DC, MC, V.*

Seafood Emporium. You'll find a good selection here of local seafood honestly prepared, plus some local specialties and live Maine lobster. Service, however, is not the best. *Royal Hawaiian Shopping Center, 2201 Kalakaua Ave., tel. 808/922–5547. Reservations recommended. Dress: casual. AC, CB, DC, MC, V.*

Steakhouse **Buzz's Steak and Lobster House.** Even though Buzz's is known for its steak, the seafood is also good and fresh. The salad bar's many delights include fresh avocado. *225 Saratoga Rd., tel. 808/923–6762. Reservations not required. Dress: casual. AE, MC, V.*

Chuck's Steak House. Basic steak and salad bar are available in a friendly setting. *Edgewater Hotel, 2168 Kalia Rd., tel. 808/923–6111 or 808/923–5866. Reservations not required. Dress: casual. AE, MC, V.*

★ **Hy's.** The chef performs behind glass in this restaurant's snug, librarylike atmosphere. Things always seem to go well at Hy's, right through to the flaming desserts. *Waikiki Park Heights Hotel, 2440 Kuhio Ave., tel. 808/922–5555. Reservations required. Dress: aloha. AE, CB, DC, MC, V.*

Inexpensive

American **Cafe Regent.** Light meals are served in an open-air setting. *Hawaiian Regent Hotel, 2552 Kalakaua Ave., tel. 808/922–6611. Reservations not required. Dress: casual. AE, CB, DC, MC, V.*

Harry's Cafe and Bar. Right in the thick of the action at the Hyatt, this sidewalk café is located in an atrium with a waterfall on the ground floor. The reasonably priced menu includes tasty sandwiches, homemade croissants, and other deli treats. Watch the passing parade and make believe you're in Paris. *Hyatt Regency Waikiki, 2424 Kalakaua Ave., tel. 808/922–9292. Reservations not required. Dress: casual. AE, CB, DC, MC, V.*

Jolly Roger East. Chow down cheaply. The breakfast pastries are delicious. *Outrigger East Hotel, 150 Kaiulani Ave., tel. 808/923–2172. Reservations not required. Dress: casual. AE, CB, DC, MC, V.*

Jolly Roger Waikiki. Same particulars as the Jolly Roger East. *2244 Kalakaua Ave., tel. 808/923–1885.*

Oceanarium. Wrapped around a huge aquarium, this one's a favorite with families. *Pacific Beach Hotel, 2490 Kalakaua Ave., tel. 808/922–1233. Reservations recommended. Dress: casual. AE, CB, DC, MC, V.*

Perry's Smorgy on Kuhio. An all-you-can-eat buffet is presented in a lovely garden setting. The site was originally designed for a first-class restaurant but Perry's got lucky. *2380 Kuhio Ave., tel. 808/926–0184. Reservations not required. Dress: casual. AE, MC, V.*

Shore Bird. A real find: You can grill your own steaks, chicken, and fish right on the beach. The restaurant has one of the best views of Diamond Head and is a good place to watch the sunset. *Outrigger Reef Hotel, 2169 Kalia Rd., tel. 808/922–2887. Reservations recommended. Dress: casual. AE, CB, DC, MC, V.*

Tony Roma's A Place For Ribs. The name says it all. *1972 Kalakaua Ave., tel. 808/942–2121. Reservations not accepted. Dress: casual. AE, MC, V.*

Wailana Coffee House. If you like coffee shops, this is a reliable one. *1869 Ala Moana Blvd., tel. 808/955–3735. Reservations not required. Dress: casual. AE, DC, MC, V.*

American/Tropical **The Beachcomber.** Polynesian atmosphere and a good menu of familiar and exotic entrées are its strengths. *Waikiki Beachcomber Hotel, 2300 Kalakaua Ave., tel. 808/922–4646. Reservations not required. Dress: casual. AE, CB, DC, MC, V.*

Chinese **Lau Yee Chai.** Although it's been billed as beautiful, this place may make you feel like you're eating in an auditorium, despite the crystal chandeliers. Visiting VIPs from mainland China head here, and it's a local favorite. *Waikiki Shopping Plaza, 2250 Kalakaua Ave., tel. 808/923–1112. Reservations recommended. Dress: casual. AE, DC, MC, V.*

German **Bavarian Beer Garden.** Boisterous, as you might expect, this restaurant has become popular in a short time. Sausage, sauerkraut, and sauerbraten, of course, are featured, along with the beer. A lively one-man band plays ballroom dance music on Waikiki's biggest floor. *Royal Hawaiian Shopping Center, 2301 Kalakaua Ave., tel. 808/922–6535. Reservations not necessary. Dress: casual. AE, MC, V.*

International **Garden Lanai.** Buffets are the specialty, and they are truly
★ bountiful, with a different dinner theme each night. Call for particulars. This is one of the best buys in Waikiki. *Queen Kapiolani Hotel, 150 Kapahulu Ave., tel. 808/922–1941. Reservations recommended for dinner. Dress: casual. AE, CB, DC, MC, V.*

Italian **Ciao!** It's lighthearted, fun fare—designer pasta and pizza. *Sheraton Waikiki, 2255 Kalakaua Ave., tel. 808/922–4422. Reservations recommended. Dress: casual. AE, CB, DC, MC, V.*

Japanese **Musashi.** It comes in many moods: communal *teppan* tables (with built-in griddles in the center), a sushi bar, and a standard dining area. Discover authentic *kaiseki* cuisine, the gourmet food of Japan, plus many dishes adapted to Western tastes, such as beginner sushi. You'll experience Japanese food without fear. *Hyatt Regency Waikiki, 2424 Kalakaua Ave., tel. 808/923–1234. Reservations recommended. Dress: casual. AE, CB, DC, MC, V.*

Seigetsu. This restaurant is always crowded with Japanese visitors, who come for the Tokyo-style udon noodles and light, flaky tempura. It gets smoky at dinner. *Waikiki Shopping Plaza, 2250 Kalakaua Ave., tel. 808/922–8686. Reservations recommended. Dress: casual. AE, DC, MC, V.*

Seafood **Ray's.** The food is good, and there are complete seafood dinners with bread, soup or salad, and rice, pasta, or red potatoes, starting at $11.95. *Waikiki Shopping Plaza, 2250 Kalakaua Ave., tel. 808/923–5717. Reservations recommended. Dress: casual. AE, DC, MC, V.*

Steakhouse **Sizzler.** There's always a special at this bargain surf 'n' turf place, with soup, salad, and hot bread. You can't beat the prices. *1945 Kalakaua Ave., tel. 808/955–4069. Reservations not accepted. Dress: casual. No credit cards.*

Restaurants near Waikiki

Very Expensive

Continental **Kamaaina Suite of the Willows Restaurant.** We're treating it as
★ a separate restaurant because it has its own kitchen. Having
been given creative freedom, Chef Kusuma Cooray shines
here. The gracious plantation-home atmosphere is enhanced
by specialty menus. *Willows Restaurant, 901 Hausten St., tel.
808/946–4808. Reservations required. Dress: aloha. AE, CB,
DC, MC, V.*

Expensive

American **The Black Orchid.** With its smart art deco decor, it's the new
"in" place. It charged $300 per couple for New Year's Eve and
not only got away with it—it was packed. People aren't required to dress up here, but everyone does. You go to be seen,
as much as to eat. Tom Selleck is one of the owners and if he's
in town, he might very well be on site. The emphasis is on fresh
seafood, including live New England lobster and homemade
pasta dishes. *Restaurant Row, 500 Ala Moana Blvd., tel. 808/
521–3111. Reservations recommended. Dress: aloha. AE, MC,
V.*

Moderate

American **Coasters.** Set outdoors on the pier near the Kalakaua Boat-
house of the Hawaii Maritime Center, this restaurant is a
definite plus in the Hawaii restaurant scene. It offers nouvelle
California cuisine with a twist—it's on the hearty side. The
seafood chowder is excellent. *Pier 7, Honolulu Harbor (across
from Restaurant Row), tel. 808/524–2233. Reservations recommended. Dress: casual. AE, DC, MC, V.*

The Willows. Thatched dining pavilions are set amid carp ponds
with prize fish. This oasis of jungle elegance features tropical
entrées, curries, and "mile-high" pies. For a glimpse of real
down-home Hawaii, reserve a space at the Thursdays-
only Kamaaina Luncheon. You'll discover lots of local food,
music, and spontaneous hula. *901 Hausten St., tel. 808/946–
4808. Reservations required. Dress: aloha. AE, CB, DC,
MC, V.*

Austro-Swiss **Alpine Village.** This unique restaurant specializes in German,
Swiss, Austrian, and other European cuisine. This local favor
ite offers complete dinners averaging $15. *2700 S. King St., tel
808/949–8889. Reservations advised. Dress: aloha. AE, DC
MC, V. Closed Sun.*

Chinese **Dynasty.** Gone is the Formica-table fast-food atmosphere so
typical of Chinese restaurants. Fine cuisine is served in a set
ting of antiques and plush Peking carpets. *Ward Warehouse
1050 Ala Moana Blvd., tel. 808/531–0208. Reservations recom
mended. Dress: aloha. AE, CB, DC, MC, V.*

Japanese **Nuuanu Onsen.** You must have a party of four or more for this
★ traditional Japanese teahouse. You'll have your own room and
gourmet Japanese delicacies served by a kimono-clad waitress
who will also teach you teahouse games after dinner. *87 Laim
Rd., tel. 808/538–9184. Reservations required at least 24 hour*

ahead. Local people book months ahead. (They'll fit you in if they can.) Dress: aloha. Bring your own liquor. No credit cards.

Steakhouse

Ruth's Chris Steak House. At last—a steakhouse that doesn't look like one. The decor is polished, pastel, and sophisticated. Salads are generous and steak cuts hefty. It also serves excellent charbroiled fish. *Restaurant Row, 500 Ala Moana Blvd., tel. 808/599–3860. Reservations recommended. Dress: aloha. AE, MC, V.*

Inexpensive

American

Hard Rock Cafe. A formula restaurant, this place is always jumping. It has mystique, but is more famous for its T-shirts than its food. *1837 Kapiolani Blvd., tel. 808/955–7383. Reservations required at lunch. No reservations accepted at dinner. Dress: casual. AE, MC, V.*

Rose City Diner. A heaping dose of nostalgia is the main course in this diner with a jukebox in every booth. Son of the famous Rose City Diner in Pasadena, it specializes in cooking just like Mom's—meat loaf and mashed potatoes, and luscious chocolate cake. Nathan's hot dogs are served, too. *Restaurant Row, 500 Ala Moana Blvd., tel. 808/524–ROSE. Reservations not necessary. Dress: Casual. No credit cards.*

Sunset Grill. The wonderful fragrance of the kiawe (a local mesquite-type wood) grill is the first thing that greets you when you enter. Specialties are grilled and rotisserie items. The ham and the salads are especially good. *Restaurant Row, 500 Ala Moana Blvd., tel. 808/521–4409. Reservations not necessary. Dress: casual. AE, MC, V.*

Chinese

★ **Hee Hing.** The busy, unpretentious atmosphere makes it feel authentic. And it is. Specialties: dim sum, Mongolian beef, drunken prawns, Peking duck. *Diamond Head Center, 449 Kapahulu Ave., tel. 808/735–5544. Reservations recommended. Dress: casual. AE, MC, V.*

★ **Maple Garden.** Its fine reputation is founded on spicy Szechuan cuisine. This restaurant isn't fancy, but all the dishes are delicious. Try the eggplant. *909 Isenberg St., tel. 808/941–6641. Reservations recommended. Dress: casual. AE, DC, MC, V.*

★ **King Tsin Restaurant.** This very popular place serves northern Chinese and Szechuan cuisine. Start off with the hot and sour soup. *1110 McCully St., tel. 808/946–3273. Reservations advised. Dress: aloha. AE, DC, MC, V.*

Italian

★ **Café Cambio.** Popular with locals, this fine restaurant specializes in authentic northern Italian contemporary cuisine. Try its famous antipasto. *1680 Kapiolani Blvd., tel. 808/942–0740. Reservations advised for lunch, no reservations for dinner. Dress: casual. MC, V. Closed Mon.*

★ **Salerno Italian Restaurant.** This fine Italian restaurant, open for lunch and dinner, is a local favorite. Generous portions of good food are served with fresh homemade bread. The special roasted pepper appetizer is wonderful. *1960 Kapiolani Blvd., tel. 808/942–5273. Reservations advised. Dress: casual. AE, DC, MC, V.*

Mexican

★ **Compadres Mexican Bar and Grill.** The after-work crowd gathers here for the frosty margaritas and good pupus. The Mexican specialties have imagination and verve. *The Ward Center,*

1200 Ala Moana Blvd., tel. 808/523–1307. Reservations not accepted. Dress: casual. AE, MC, V.

Mixed Menu **Kaimuki Inn.** The food is such a chop suey mixture of Asian and American dishes that it's hard to categorize it. The lunch buffet is about the best bargain in town at $6.95. Soup and a make-your-own frozen yogurt sundae are included. *3579 Waialae Ave., tel. 808/732–3437. Reservations recommended. Dress: casual. MC, V.*

Thai **Keo's.** Hollywood celebrities have discovered this twinkling
★ nook, with tables set amid lighted trees and big paper umbrellas. The food is exceptional. Favorites: Evil Jungle Prince and Chiang Mai salad. Ask for them mild; they'll still be hot, but not as hot as they could be. The crispy noodles have a wonderful, barely there sauce. Food comes in serving dishes, Chinese style. *625 Kapahulu Ave., tel. 808/737–8240. Reservations required. Dress: casual. AC, CB, DC, MC, V.*

Picnics

You may want to pack a picnic supper or take along a picnic lunch on an excursion. Here are some suggestions:

Chez Sushi (Ward Center, 1200 Ala Moana Blvd., tel. 808/536–1007). It's all sushi, in a wide variety, and a picnic platter is available. The Supreme is big enough for two and includes California roll. Cost: $16. No delivery.

The Gourmet Deli (Manoa Marketplace, tel. 808/988–3013). Specialties are deli meats, salads, pâtés, quiches, and chocolate cake. Cost: $20–$25 for two, plus a $5 delivery charge to Waikiki.

King's Bakery (444 Hobron La., Eaton Sq., tel. 808/973–9704). Specialty: local plate lunch packed in foam containers. The bakery products are good, too. The Hawaiian Sweet Bread is a popular souvenir. Cost: up to $5.95 per person. No delivery.

Shirokiya (Ala Moana Shopping Center, upper level, tel. 808/941–9111). Pick from a mind-boggling selection of Japanese *bento* (boxed) lunches, all packed and ready to go. Cost: $2.50–$8.25. No delivery.

Tad and Pat (3154 Waialae Ave., at Third Ave., Kaimuki, tel. 808/735–1747). This top catering company will pack a special picnic with chilled wine, picnic cloth, roses, and a gourmet food assortment. Cost: $50 for two, plus a $30 charge for delivery to your Waikiki hotel.

8 Lodging

Introduction

There are places in the world as sunny as Waikiki, and some where the beach is just about as good. As for those waving palms, they sprout like weeds in the tropics. The factor that sets Hawaii apart from its resort competitors is the service—in other words, the people with whom you come in contact every day. Their hospitality is part of the aloha spirit, and their training is often done at the college level. Tourism is their profession. In this regard, Hawaii is more like Europe than the United States. Hospitality is a respected career, drawing top talent—people who have pride in what they do.

Hotel properties in Waikiki range from ultradeluxe, with palatial appointments, to tropical tacky. Some are on the beach and some are blocks away with a view of no more than a neighbor's air conditioner. Some people look at a hotel as simply a place to sleep at night. Others prefer a bit of ambience. The hotels that are recommended in each price category reflect a bias for atmosphere. A place doesn't have to be expensive to be clean, friendly, and attractive. For a complete list of every hotel and condominium unit in the state, write to the Hawaii Visitors Bureau for the free *Accommodation Guide*. It details amenities and gives each hotel's proximity to the beach.

If you want a hotel right on the beach, ask for it. Don't be fooled by sleek expensive brochures. A sharp photographer can find an angle to make almost any hotel look like it's right on the ocean. Hawaiian lawmakers showed foresight when they prohibited the sale of beaches to private parties. As a result, all beaches are open to the public, and most have convenient public access protected by law. You don't have to pay a premium to stay in a hotel near the beach. You can rent a little room three blocks away from the ocean and spend your days in the sand sitting right next to the hundred-dollar-a-day crowd.

Except for the peak months of February and August, you'll have no trouble getting a room. When making your reservations, either on your own or through a travel agent, ask about packages and extras. Some hotels have special tennis, golf, or honeymoon packages. Others have periodic room and car packages.

The most highly recommended hotels in each price category are indicated by a star ★.

Category	Cost*
Very Expensive	over $125
Expensive	$90–$125
Moderate	$50–$90
Inexpensive	under $50

double room; add 9¼% taxes, plus service

The following credit card abbreviations are used: AE, American Express; CB, Carte Blanche; DC, Diners Club; MC, MasterCard; and V, Visa. Waikiki hotel prices usually follow a European plan, meaning no meals included.

Very Expensive

Aston Waikiki Beach Tower. Oriental screens and warm wood make the lobby seem like a private living room in this all-suites hotel. Suites are tastefully decorated. Colors are light, everything is coordinated, and all the pleasant little touches, such as baskets and centerpieces, are in place. *2470 Kalakaua Ave., Honolulu 96815, tel. 808/926–6400 or 800/367–5124; in Canada 800/423–8733. Across the street from the beach. 140 suites with bath, kitchen, wet bar. Facilities: paddle tennis, heated pool, jet spa, sauna, 3 meeting rooms. AE, CB, DC, MC, V.*

★ **Colony Surf Hotel.** This establishment is like a condominium, with each unit having a full kitchen and an attractive living area. The same is true of the hotel's annex, the **Colony Surf East,** but units in the Colony Surf are more spacious. The Colony Surf is small, with impeccable and personal service. The staff will even hold your aloha shirts and beach paraphernalia until your next visit. Wealthy patrons like to keep this one a secret. It's way up on the Diamond Head end of Waikiki, beyond the mainstream. Its restaurant, Michel's, is French, fashionable, and open to the sea. It is considered to be the most romantic dining room in town. *2895 Kalakaua Ave., Honolulu 96815, tel. 808/923–5751 or 800/367–6046. On the beach. Of 171 units, 50 function as hotel units. There are an additional 50 units in the Colony Surf East. Facilities: 3 restaurants, 3 cocktail lounges in both buildings. No pool. AE, CB, DC, MC, V.*

Diamond Head Beach Hotel. Right on the ocean, this hotel also sits at the quiet end of Waikiki. Many of the rooms, decorated by a popular Los Angeles design firm, have an emphasis on mirrors, glass, and fine fabrics. Some rooms have kitchenettes. Continental breakfast is served to all guests. *2947 Kalakaua Ave., Honolulu 96815, tel. 808/922–1928 or 800/367– 6046. Of a total of 60 units, 56 are hotel units. No pool. AE, CB, DC, MC, V.*

★ **Halekulani.** Sleek, modern, and luxurious, the marble and wood rooms all have lanais, sitting areas, refrigerators, bathrobes, and dozens of little touches that spell pamper. The in-room check-in service means no waiting in the lobby. The deluxe Halekulani was built around the garden lanai and historic 1931 building of the gracious old Halekulani. The hotel has two of the finest restaurants in Honolulu and an oceanside pool with a giant orchid mosaic. *2199 Kalia Rd., Honolulu 96815, tel. 808/923–2311 or 800/367–2343. On the beach. 456 rooms with bath. Facilities: swimming pool, shops, meeting rooms, 3 restaurants, 1 lounge. AE, CB, DC, MC, V.*

★ **Hyatt Regency Waikiki.** The focal point of this twin-towered beauty is the 10-story atrium lobby with a two-story waterfall and a mammoth metal sculpture. With shops, concerts, and Harry's Bar, this is one of the liveliest lobbies anywhere, though you may get lost in it. The Hyatt is known for several fine restaurants: glamorous Bagwells 2424, the Japanese Musashi, Italian Spats, and the Colony Steak House. With two towers, there are two Regency Clubs and eight penthouses. *2424 Kalakaua Ave., Honolulu 96815, tel. 808/923–1234 or 800/ 228–9000. Across the street from the beach. 1,234 rooms. Facilities: 6 restaurants; 6 lounges, including a disco and a jazz club; a swimming pool; 70 shops. AE, CB, DC, MC, V.*

★ **Kahala Hilton.** This hotel is not technically in Waikiki, but it is literally minutes away on the quiet side of Diamond Head, in

Lodging

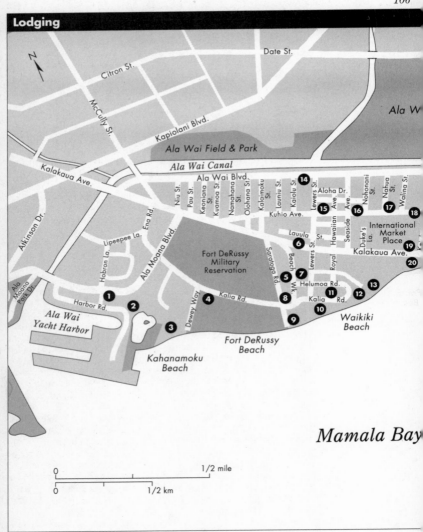

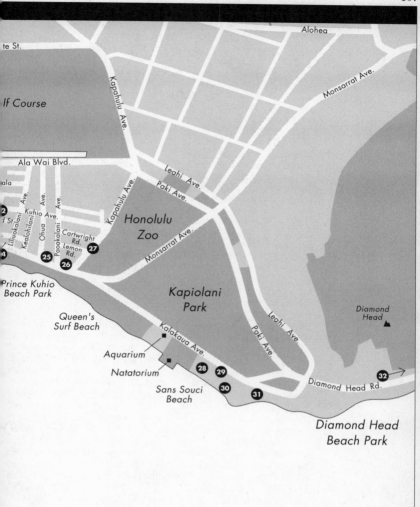

the wealthy residential neighborhood of Kahala. Here's where kings, Hollywood stars, and presidents stay. Elegant and understated, the Kahala Hilton has a porpoise pond, plus four distinguished restaurants and a supper club featuring local star Danny Kaleikini. The staff prides itself on its service. The hotel's private Maunalua Bay Health and Tennis Club is a short shuttle away. *5000 Kahala Ave., Honolulu 96816, tel. 808/734–2211 or 800/367–2525. On the beach. 319 rooms and suites plus 84 cottage-style units in the Lagoon Terrace. Facilities: swimming pool, tennis court, shops, meeting rooms, 4 restaurants, 2 lounges. AE, CB, DC, MC, V.*

★ **Royal Hawaiian Hotel.** The Pink Palace of the Pacific was built in 1927, in an age of gracious and leisurely travel when people sailed on the Matson luxury liners and spent months at the Royal. Echoing that grand era, the hotel has high ceilings, period furniture, and flowered wallpaper. Some people have been coming here for 30 years and insist on a favorite chair or bureau. The hotel has a storeroom full of old furniture that it dares not throw away because the pieces move in and out with nostalgic guests. Dreams are made of breakfast at the beachside Surf Room, the corridors of pink carpeting, and the great crystal chandeliers tinkling in the wind. The new modern wing is more expensive, but for charm, the original building can't be beat. *2259 Kalakaua Ave., Honolulu 96815, tel. 808/923–7311 or 800/325–3535. On the beach. 527 rooms. Facilities: swimming pool, meeting rooms, 2 restaurants, 2 lounges. AE, CB, DC, MC, V.*

★ **Sheraton Moana Surfrider.** The marvelous old building, erected in 1901, is Waikiki's oldest hotel. Sheraton has taken great pains and spent millions to restore this landmark structure to its former grandeur. The Moana has merged with the Surfrider, next door. Both have a unified decor theme, based on the architectural features of the old Moana, specifically the arched windows. Rooms in the old Moana section (ask for the Diamond Wing or the Banyan Wing) have big wide windows. Many of the rooms appear to be right on the sand. Period decor includes armoires that house television, minibar, and safe. At first glance, the bathrooms look delightfully old-fashioned, but a second look reveals lighted makeup mirrors and modern amenities. Rooms are short on closet space. If that's important to you, stay in the Tower Wing (former Surfrider section). *2365 Kalakaua Ave., Honolulu 96815, tel 808/922–3111 or 800/325–3535. On the beach. 793 rooms. Facilities: swimming pool, shops, meeting rooms, restaurants, and lounges (number undetermined at press time). AE, CB, DC, MC, V.*

Expensive

Hawaiian Regent Hotel. The huge lobbies and courtyards, open to the breezes, are sunlit and contemporary in feel. With two towers and two lobbies, the layout is a bit confusing. If you can get past that, this is an outstanding hotel. It has several dining choices, including the award-winning Third Floor Restaurant, now known as **The Secret**, and two Japanese restaurants. *2552 Kalakaua Ave., Honolulu 96815, tel. 808/922–6611 or 800/367–5370. Across the street from the beach. 1,346 rooms with bath. Facilities: shops, meeting rooms, 2 swimming pools, 1 tennis court, 2 lounges, 1 disco, 5 restaurants. AE, CB, DC, MC, V.*

★ **Hilton Hawaiian Village.** Hilton spent $100 million to remake this complex into a brand-new, lavishly landscaped resort, the largest in the state. There are four towers, five restaurants, three swimming pools, and a botanical garden of labeled flora that is home to a collection of rare, beautiful avifauna. The hotel has its own dock for its catamaran and a fine stretch of oceanfront. The top floor and the lower floors of the Rainbow Tower tend to be noisy. Dining options include the award-winning Bali and the fine Chinese food at Golden Dragon. *2005 Kalia Rd., Honolulu 96815, tel. 808/949–4321 or 800/HIL-TONS. On the beach. 2,524 rooms. Facilities: 2-tier super-pool(10,000 sq.ft.), 2 additional swimming pools, 5 restaurants, and 5 lounges. AE, CB, DC, MC, V.*

Holiday Inn-Waikiki Beach. It's almost next to Kapiolani Park, with the zoo and other attractions. The best sunset views are from the wall in front of the hotel. Rooms are on the low end of the expensive range. *2570 Kalakaua Ave., Honolulu 96815, tel. 808/922–2511 or 800/877–7666. Across the street from the beach. 714 rooms. Facilities: swimming pool, 2 restaurants, 3 lounges, and a shop. AE, CB, DC, MC, V.*

Ilikai Waikiki Hotel. This is the tennis center of Waikiki, and also the closest hotel to the famous Ala Moana Shopping Center and the popular Ala Moana Beach Park. There are three towers and a huge esplanade, which is always busy; crowds usually gather to watch hula dancing demonstrations and local musicians. You can get a good look at the Ala Wai Yacht Harbor, and the best view of Waikiki is from Annabelle's lounge atop the hotel. *1777 Ala Moana Blvd., Honolulu 96815, tel. 808/949–3811 or 800/228–3000. Not on the beach. 800 rooms. Facilities: 2 swimming pools, 7 tennis courts, meeting rooms, shops, 5 restaurants, 2 lounges. AE, CB, DC, MC, V.*

Outrigger Reef Hotel. Recently renovated, this hotel has a tile porte-cochere (carriage entrance) that looks like the luxurious Halekulani Hotel next door. There's a waterscape and lots of greenery. Most guest rooms have new light furniture and spreads. The Diamond Head suites have great views. Most rooms have small lanais. *2169 Kalia Rd., Honolulu 96815, tel. 808/923–3111 or 800/ 367–5170; in Canada 800/826–6786. 883 rooms. Facilities: swimming pool, 4 restaurants, lounges, shops, meeting rooms. AE, DC, MC, V.*

Princess Kaiulani Hotel. Sheraton service, charging privileges, and refurbished rooms make this a good choice, though it's a block from the beach. *120 Kaiulani Ave., Honolulu 96815, tel. 808/922–5811 or 800/325–3535. 1,156 rooms. Facilities: swimming pool, 4 restaurants, lounge. AE, CB, DC, MC, V.*

Sheraton Waikiki. This establishment towers over its neighbors. It was recently refurbished in tones of periwinkle and peach, which look much too sedate in a building of such extravagant proportions. Fortunately, the gigantic capiz-shell chandeliers that clatter in the trade winds have been maintained. The rooms are spacious, many with grand views of Diamond Head. The hotel is located right in the thick of things. *2255 Kalakaua Ave., Honolulu 96815, tel. 808/922–4422 or 800/ 325–3535. On the beach. 1,852 rooms. Facilities: 2 swimming pools, shops, meeting rooms, 4 restaurants, 3 lounges. AE, CB, DC, MC, V.*

Waikiki Joy. A new boutique hotel in the heart of Waikiki, it has a breezy white-marble entry. This is Yuppie heaven with a Jacuzzi and remote-control stereo system in each tastefully decorated room. *320 Lewers St., Honolulu 96815, tel. 808/923–2300 or 800/733–5569. Not on the beach. 101 rooms. Facilities:*

small swimming pool, lounge, restaurant. AE, CB, DC, MC, V.

★ **Waikiki Parc.** The hotel bills itself as "affordable luxury." Everything lives up to that premise except the main entrance, which is down a narrow side street. The lobby is light with mirrors and pastel tones. Guest rooms are done in cool blues and whites, with lots of rattan. Some rooms are in the expensive category, but many start as low as $90. The hotel has a fine Japanese restaurant, Kacho. *22–33 Helumoa Rd., Honolulu 96815, tel. 808/921–7272 or 800/422–0450. Not on the beach. 298 rooms with bath. Facilities: swimming pool, 2 restaurants, 2 shops. AE, CB, DC, MC, V.*

Moderate

★ **Aston Waikikian on the Beach.** It's one of the few low-rise hotels left, although it does have a newer air-conditioned Tiki Tower. The Tahitian Lanai restaurant has a faithful local following. This hotel is a little gem, unpolished perhaps, in spots, but the romance of old Hawaii is definitely here, in the South-Seas style architecture with high-pitched roofs and the jungle-like gardens. Not technically on the beach, it fronts the Duke Kahanamoku Lagoon with a sandy shore. *1811 Ala Moana Blvd.,Honolulu 96815, tel. 808/949–5331 or 800/922–7866; in Canada 800/268–7866. 132 rooms. Facilities: swimming pool, shops, restaurant, cocktail lounge. AE, CB, DC, MC, V.*

The Breakers. This old, quiet sleeper of a hotel, with its gardens and pool, is an oasis in a busy area of Waikiki. Its low-rise units are set amid tropical flora, and all have kitchenettes. *250 Beach Walk, Honolulu 96815, tel. 808/923–3181 or 800/426–0494. 66 rooms. Facility: swimming pool. AE, MC, V.*

★ **Coconut Plaza Waikiki.** There couldn't be a prettier hotel in the price range. A waterfall cascades into the lobby swimming pool. Mexican tile floors and pale furniture keep the guest rooms looking cool. Only drawback: small bathrooms with showers only; no tubs. *2171 The Ala Wai, Honolulu 96815, tel. 808/923–8828 or 800/882–9696. Not on the beach. 86 rooms. Facilities: swimming pool, restaurant and lounge. MC, V.*

New Otani Kaimana Beach. This establishment has come a long way. The ambience is cheerful and charming. Completely revamped, the lobby is open and airy with new light-colored tiles. Guest rooms have all been redone, most of them in pastel tones. Best of all, the hotel is right on the beach at the quiet end of Waikiki, practically at the foot of Diamond Head. Hotel manager Steve Boyle has received national recognition for his efforts to preserve the beauty of Diamond Head and often leads hikes to the summit. Ask about them when you check in. The outdoor Hau Tree Lanai is one of the nicest seaside restaurants around, and it's often overlooked by the throngs who go for the fancier places. *2863 Kalakaua Ave., Honolulu 96815, tel. 808/923–1555 or 800/657–7949; in CA 800/252–0197; in Canada 800/421–8795. 138 rooms. Facilities: 2 restaurants (1 Japanese), a lounge, shops, meeting rooms; no pool. AE, CB, DC, MC, V.*

Outrigger East. The public areas aren't much to look at, but the rooms are spacious; if you're above the 12th floor, you'll be able to see all the way to Diamond Head. Insist on a view when booking. The upper rooms are one of Waikiki's bargains. *150 Kaiulani Ave., Honolulu 96815, tel. 808/922–5777 or 800/367–5170; in Canada 800/826–6786. Not on the beach. 444 rooms.*

Facilities: a swimming pool, 4 restaurants, 4 lounges. AE, CB, DC, MC, V.

Outrigger Surf. It's agreeable for its price range. The pool is tiny, but the deluxe rooms are surprisingly commodious. *2280 Kuhio Ave., Honolulu 96815, tel. 808/922–5777 or 800/367–5170; Canada 800/826–6786. Not on the beach. 251 rooms. Facilities: swimming pool, restaurant, cocktail lounge. AE, CB, DC, MC, V.*

Outrigger West. Everything about this hotel is tidy and compact. Most rooms have kitchenettes, so if you're counting pennies, ask for one. *2330 Kuhio Ave., Honolulu 96815, tel. 808/922–5022 or 800/367–5170; in Canada 800/826–6786. Not on the beach. 660 rooms. Facilities: swimming pool, 2 restaurants, 2 lounges. AE, CB, DC, MC, V.*

Queen Kapiolani Hotel. With its light buff exterior that almost blends with the sidewalk it fronts, this hotel can easily be missed, even if you're looking for it. If you hear lions roaring from the zoo across the street, you're getting warm. The Queen Kapiolani is often overlooked, but it doesn't deserve to be. Among its virtues are an excellent location, across the street from Kapiolani Park and a half-block from the beach, plus a restaurant serving one of the best nightly buffets in town. *150 Kapahulu Ave., Honolulu 96815, tel. 808/922–1941 or 800/367–5004. 315 rooms. Facilities: swimming pool, restaurant, lounge, shops, meeting room. AE, CB, DC, MC, V.*

Inexpensive

Coral Seas Hotel. Beauty is not its business; bargains are. Located right in the heart of Waikiki, it has no pool but does boast a Perry's Smorgy all-you-can-eat restaurant. For simply eating and sleeping cheaply, it's okay; just be on the beach early and stay late. *250 Lewers St., Honolulu 96815, tel. 808/923–3881 or 800/367–5170; in Canada 800/826–6786. Not on the beach. 109 rooms. Facilities: 2 restaurants, lounge, shops. AE, CB, DC, MC, V.*

Hale Koa Hotel. If you're lucky enough to be active or retired military personnel or a dependent (and can prove it), this is the best deal in Waikiki. Otherwise, this hotel is strictly off-limits. *2055 Kalia Rd., Honolulu 96815, tel. 808/955–0555 or 800/367–6027. On the beach. 420 rooms. Facilities: swimming pool, tennis courts, restaurants, lounges, meeting rooms, shops. AE, CB, DC, MC, V.*

Malihini Hotel. There's no pool, no air-conditioning in any of the units, and the rooms are spartan. Still, the atmosphere of this low-rise complex is cool and pleasant, and the gardens are well-maintained. *217 Saratoga Rd., Honolulu 96815, tel. 808/923–9644. Not on the beach. 29 rooms with kitchenettes. Facilities: 1 shop. No credit cards.*

Royal Grove Hotel. It's hard to go wrong in this flamingo-pink hotel, reminiscent of Miami. The lobby is comfortable; the rooms are agreeably furnished, each with a kitchenette; and the pool area is bright with tropical flora. Most people enjoy the family atmosphere. *151 Uluniu Ave., Honolulu 96815, tel. 808/923–7691. Not on the beach. 87 rooms. Facilities: swimming pool. AE, CB, DC, MC, V.*

Waikiki Circle Hotel. If you look out at the view instead of in at the small rooms, this silo-shaped hotel is okay for the money. *2464 Kalakaua Ave., Honolulu 96815, tel. 808/923–1571. 104* *rooms. Facilities: restaurant, lounge; no pool. AE, CB, DC, MC, V.*

Waikiki Surf Hotel. The lower floors are noisy, and while some rooms are well furnished and decorated, others need a face-lift. Ask for an upper floor and have your room changed if you don't like it. Many rooms have kitchenettes. This is a good find. *2200 Kuhio Ave., Honolulu 96815, tel. 808/923-7671 or 800/367-5170. 291 rooms. Facilities: swimming pool, lounge, shops. AE, CB, DC, MC, V.*

Bed-and-Breakfast

Two bed-and-breakfast bookers actually offer homestays in and around Waikiki in the moderate range. Both companies are reliable, have been in business a number of years, and have a good inventory of units. **Bed and Breakfast Honolulu** has an especially good selection of Waikiki rooms, including a place to stay in one of the few remaining private homes in Waikiki.

Bed and Breakfast Honolulu, 3242 Kaohinani Dr., Honolulu 96817, tel. 808/595-7533; from the U.S. Mainland, tel. 800/288-4666.

Pacific Hawaii Bed and Breakfast, 19 Kai Nani Pl., Kailua 96734, tel. 808/262-6026.

9 The Arts and Nightlife

Waikiki nightlife can be as simple as a barefoot stroll in the sand or as elaborate as a dinner show with all the spangles and long-legged choreography of a Las Vegas gig. You can take a sunset cruise and view a seascape of scintillating color, or let a bus whisk you from bustling Waikiki to a remote beach for a luau.

Kalakaua and Kuhio avenues come to life when the lights go on. It's fun just to people-watch. Some strollers know right where they're going—they've got reservations. Others wander along reading every sign, every posted menu—looking for something to strike their fancy—the right enticement, the right price, or maybe a hummable song. There's plenty of latitude for serendipity. To use the argot of youth, "Hawaii is laid back." Hawaiian time is any time.

Wafting through all the after-dark activities is the sound of music of every kind—from classical to country. Music has been the language of Hawaii from the beginning. Lacking a written language, the ancients spoke through music. The chants and dances recorded history and genealogy. They spoke of royal affairs of the heart, gods, legends, and great deeds. Music also entertained. When the missionaries arrived with their *himeni* (hymns), the Hawaiians took the new rhythms to their souls.

Today, there's a new music in the soul of Hawaii. Rock and disco have asserted themselves and been synthesized into the local music pool. There are strong currents of jazz and, lately, country music. Traditional Hawaiian music has evolved into a contemporary sound, with a great respect, bordering on reverence, for the older forms.

You can find it all in Waikiki. The hula comes in sequined skirts or authentic ti-leaf skirts. There are ipu drums and electric guitars, mercifully not on the same stage in most cases. The latest high-tech, ultrastereo video discos are here, side by side with the ukulele trio.

In addition, Honolulu has a symphony orchestra, an opera company, and a chamber music group. The star ballet troupes also come gliding through. Check the local newspapers, the *Honolulu Star Bulletin* or the *Honolulu Advertiser*.

The Arts

Theater

The **Honolulu Community Theater** (tel. 808/734–0274), is in residence five minutes from Waikiki at Fort Ruger Theater on Diamond Head. The 75-year-old group stages outstanding musicals, comedies, and dramas, using both professional talent and talented amateurs. Performances are offered year-round. Tickets: $10–$17.50.

The **John F. Kennedy Theater** (tel. 808/948–7655), at the University of Hawaii East-West Center campus in Manoa, is the setting for theater productions, Kabuki, Noh, and Chinese opera. Check local newspapers for programs.

University theater. There are active drama programs at the University of Hawaii, Chaminade College, Brigham Young University–Hawaii Campus, and Hawaii Loa College.

The **Honolulu Theater for Youth** (HTY) stages delightful productions for children around the state, July–May. For a schedule, contact HTY (1100 Alakea St., Suite 333, Honolulu 96813, tel. 808/521–3487). Tickets: $6 adults, $4 youth.

Manoa Valley Theatre offers wonderful amateur productions in an intimate theater in Manoa Valley. Contact HPAC (2833 E. Manoa Rd., Honolulu 96822, tel. 808/988–6131). Its season is September–June. Tickets: $9–$14 at the box office.

Music

The Hawaii Opera Theater's season runs February–March. Performances at Blaisdell Concert Hall (Ward Ave. and King St., tel. 808/521–6537). The 1991 schedule features *Aida, Candide,* and *The Marriage of Figaro.* Performances are Tuesday, Friday, and Sunday, with preview lectures at the Honolulu Academy of Arts the week before each performance.

The Honolulu Symphony's season runs September–April, Tuesday evenings and Sunday afternoons (Blaisdell Concert Hall, Ward Ave. and King St.). The Symphony on the Light Side series is on Friday evenings during the same season. Island musicians are often featured with the symphony. During the summer, the popular Starlight series is performed outdoors at the Waikiki Shell, Kapiolani Park. For a schedule, write or phone the Honolulu Symphony Society (1441 Kapiolani Blvd., Honolulu, tel. 808/942–2200).

Chamber Music Hawaii (tel. 808/531–6617) gives 25 concerts a year at the Lutheran Church (1730 Punahou St.), Honolulu Academy of Arts (Beretania St. and Ward Ave.), and at other locations around the island.

During the school year, faculty concerts of the **University of Hawaii Music Dept.** (tel. 808/948–7756) are held at Orvis Auditorium on campus.

Rock concerts are usually performed at Neal Blaisdell Center Arena (tel. 808/521–2911). The megastars pack them in at Aloha Stadium (tel. 808/488–7731).

Films

Art films. Art, international, old classic, and silent films are consistently screened at the little theater at the **Honolulu Academy of Arts** (Beretania St. and Ward Ave.). The theater entrance is around the back on Kinau Street. For film information, tel. 808/538–1006. Dinner is served Thursday at 6:30 PM. Reservations are necessary (tel. 808/531–8865).

The Varsity Theater (1106 University Ave., tel. 808/946–4144) brings in internationally acclaimed pictures.

The Hawaii International Film Festival (tel. 808/944–7666) may not be Cannes, but it is unique and exciting. It is based on the theme "When Strangers Meet." Top films from the United States, Asia, and the Pacific are aired day and night at several theaters on Oahu during the week-long festival. Many local people plan their vacations around this time and spend days viewing free films and attending lectures, workshops, and social events. Scheduled for late November through early December.

Dance

Every autumn, the Honolulu Symphony Society brings in the **San Francisco Ballet.** Telephone 808/537–6161 or write to the Symphony Society (*see* Music, above). **Ballet Hawaii** (tel. 808/ 988–7578), a local company, is active during the holiday season with its annual *Nutcracker* production at the Mamiya Theater, Chaminade University.

Nightlife

The drinking age in Hawaii is 21, although many bars admit younger people without serving them alcohol. By law, all establishments that serve alcoholic beverages must close at 2 AM. The only exceptions are those with a cabaret license, which have a 4 AM curfew. Even though they may be billed as a discothèque, they are required to have live music. All listings below are in Waikiki unless noted. Most have a cover charge of $2–$4.

Dancing

Annabelle's (Ilikai Waikiki Hotel, 1777 Ala Moana Blvd., tel. 808/949–3811). It offers disco dancing atop the hotel with Honolulu city lights spread out below. This spot attracts a casual crowd, which may be classified as the "beer bunch." Nightly 9–4.

The Black Orchid is Honolulu's newest trendy scene. Gentlemen don't have to wear a jacket here, but almost everyone does. The music is excellent, the place stylish, and it's comfortable for both singles and couples (*see* Restaurants near Waikiki in Chapter 7). Weeknights 5:30 PM–1:30 AM, Sat. 8:30 PM–3:30 AM, Sun. 9 PM–3:30 AM.

Bobby McGee's Conglomeration (2885 Kalakaua Ave., tel. 808/ 922–1282). Disco dancing for younger adults in the 21–30 age group. Nightly 7–2.

Esprit (Sheraton Waikiki Hotel, 2255 Kalakaua Ave., tel. 808/ 922–4422). Disco dancing. Bernadette and Sunshine Company Tues.–Sat. Love Notes Sun.–Mon. Tourists flock here, and so do local men looking for tourist women. Nightly 9–1.

Katz Disco (870 Kapahulu Ave., near Waikiki, tel. 808/737–4661). The latest in recorded music, plus a good selection of nonalcoholic beverages. This is for a very young crowd. Teen dances Mon.–Thurs. nights 9–2; Mon.–Sat. nights 9–2.

Maharaja (2255 Kuhio Ave., tel. 808/922–3030). Disco dancing nightly 5–2.

Maile Lounge (Kahala Hilton Hotel, 5000 Kahala Ave., tel. 808/ 734–2211). Mellow music and a small intimate dance floor make this a romantic spot. Nightly 8–midnight.

Masquerade Club (224 McCully St., near Waikiki, tel. 808/949–6337). Video dancing. Nightly 9–4; teen party Fri.–Sat. 6–9.

Monarch Room (Royal Hawaiian Hotel, 2255 Kalakaua Ave., tel. 808/923–7311). Dancing to the big-band sound of Del Courtney. Dancers spill outside near the ocean. Sun. night 4:30–8:30.

Nick's Fishmarket (Waikiki Gateway Hotel, 2070 Kalakaua Ave., tel. 808/955–6333). This is probably the most comfortable of the dance lounges, with an elegant crowd, inspiring music, and an intimate, dark atmosphere. There's some singles action here. Wed.–Sat. 9–1:30.

Nicholas Nickolas (Ala Moana Hotel, 410 Atkinson Dr., near Waikiki, tel. 808/955–4466). The view is splendid, the music is good, and the crowd dresses well. This one has grown in popularity with the local Yuppie crowd. Dancing Sun.–Thurs. nights 9:30–2:15; Fri.–Sat. nights 10–3:15.

Paradise Lounge (Hilton Hawaiian Village, 2005 Kalia Rd., tel. 808/949–4321). It's expensive and reflected in the crowd. Dancing Sun.–Thurs. 6:30–10:30, Fri.–Sat. 8:30–12:30.

The Pink Cadillac (478 Ena Rd., tel. 808/942–5282). Nightly dancing, with a restaurant for light snacks. Sunday is Beach Party Night, and Thursday ladies get in free. Nightly 9–2.

Point After (Hawaiian Regent Hotel, 2552 Kalakaua Ave., tel. 808/922–6611). Dance Revue Tues.–Sat. 9–10:30. Nightly dancing 10:30–4.

Rumours (Ala Moana Hotel, 410 Atkinson St., tel. 808/955–4811). It's just been completely redone with all the latest lights and video effects for disco dancing. It draws the more sophisticated after-work crowd. Sun.–Thurs. nights 5–2, Fri.–Sat. nights 5–4.

Scruples (Waikiki Market Place, 2310 Kuhio Ave., tel. 808/923–9530). Disco dancing to the top 40, with a young adult, mostly local crowd. Nightly 8–4.

Spats (Hyatt Regency Waikiki, 2424 Kalakaua Ave., tel. 808/923–1234). Disco dancing in a speakeasy atmosphere. Dance contest with a $200 prize Mon., singing contest Wed., bikini contest Wed., hi-tech flirtation contest Fri., fashion auction Sun. A real mix of people gathers in this pleasant, though loud, place. Nightly 9–4.

Rock

Moose McGillycuddys Pub and Cafe (310 Lewers St., tel. 808/923–0751). Live Band plays for the beach-and-beer gang. Light snacks are served. Nightly 9–1:30.

Wave Waikiki (1877 Kalakaua Ave., tel. 808/941–0424). Dance to live rock 'n' roll until 1:30, recorded music after that. It can be a rough scene. Nightly 9–4.

Jazz

Trappers (Hyatt Regency Waikiki, 2424 Kalakaua Ave., tel. 808/922–9292). Trappers is an elegant night spot featuring such popular musicians as The New Orleans Jazz Band. Nightly 5–2.

Shows

Some entertainers have been around for years, others are new on the scene. Generally, the dinner-show food is acceptable, what you might expect to get at a political dinner, and not much more. The two notable exceptions are the **Monarch Room of the Royal Hawaiian Hotel,** where the Brothers Cazimero are in residence, and the **Hala Terrace of the Kahala Hilton,** where Danny Kaleikini has been reigning for more than 20 years. In both places, the dinner is enjoyable. If you want to dine on your own and take in a show, sign up for a cocktail show. Dinner shows are all in the $35–$45 range, with the cocktail shows running $17–$25. The prices usually include one cocktail, tax, and gratuity.

Al Harrington (Polynesian Palace, Reef Towers Hotel, 247 Lewers St., tel. 808/923–9861). Harrington is a singer with a rich voice and a cast of 16 musicians and dancers to back him up. Reservations required. Sun.–Fri. First dinner show 5; first cocktail show seating 5:45. Second dinner seating 8; second cocktail seating 8:30.

Brothers Cazimero (Royal Hawaiian Hotel, 2259 Kalakaua Ave., tel. 808/923–7311). This is a class act appearing in the beautiful Monarch Room. The music is a splendid blend of traditional and contemporary Hawaiian tunes. Even the dinner is good. Dinner show Tues.–Sat. 7, additional cocktail show Fri.–Sat. 10:30.

Danny Kaleikini (Kahala Hilton Hotel, 5000 Kahala Ave., tel. 808/734–2211). The mood is mellow. Kaleikini's a gentleman, and a very gifted one. Book early for this one. There's rarely an empty table. Dinner show Mon.–Sat. 7.

Don Ho (The Dome, Hilton Hawaiian Village, 2005 Kalia Rd., tel. 808/949–4321). Waikiki's old pro still packs them in with a glitzy Vegas-style Polynesian revue. Reservations required. Dinner seating 6:30, cocktail seating 7:45.

Flashback (Hula Hut Theater Restaurant, 286 Beach Walk, tel. 808/923–8411). Elvis Presley look-alike pours on the nostalgia. The Elvis imitator looks pretty close to the real thing. Dinner show Mon.–Sat. 8.

Polynesian Cultural Center (55–370 Kamehameha Hwy., Laie, tel. 808/293–3333). Easily one of the best shows in the Islands. Actors are students from Brigham Young University–Hawaii Campus. The show has soaring moments and an "erupting" volcano. Dinner from 4:30; show 7:30.

"Kamaaina Friday Night" (Sea Life Park, Makapuu Point, tel. 808/259–7933). A musical revue is staged at this marine park and is covered by the park admission of $12.95. This show is most enjoyable if planned during an afternoon at the park. Stay for dinner in the restaurant (not included in the admission). Transportation from Waikiki: Bus No. 58. Special shuttle returns to Waikiki after the show.

Society of Seven (Waikiki Outrigger Hotel, 2335 Kalakaua Ave., tel. 808/922–6408). A lively, popular group that has great staying power and an upbeat contemporary sound. Mon.–Sat. 8:30 and 10:30. One 8:30 show on Wed.

Tropics Surf Club (Hilton Hawaiian Village, 2005 Kalia Rd., tel. 808/942–7873). Charo, the famous Cootchie-Cootchie girl, has been packing them in Monday through Saturday with a humorous and vivacious show that keeps the audience clapping and happy. Dinner Show starts at 6:45 for $44.50. Cocktail Show starts at 7:45 for $24.50.

The Luau

Just about everyone who comes to Hawaii goes to at least one luau. Originally, the traditional luau would last for days with feasting, sporting events, hula, and song. Today's version is scaled down and, for the most part, not authentic. You're as likely to find macaroni salad on the buffet next to the poi and big heaps of fried chicken beside the platter of kalua pig. Some things that visitors actually enjoy are laulau, lomilomi salmon, and haupia (*see* Chapter 7 for Hawaiian food definitions). As for notorious poi, the clean bland taste goes nicely with something salty, like bacon or kalua pig with salt.

If you want authenticity, look in the newspaper to see if a church or civic club is holding a luau fundraiser. You'll not only be welcome, you'll see some down-home Hawaiiana.

If you'll settle for fun without much thought to tradition, here are some other good luaus. They cost $40–$50 for adults; $30 for children.

Germaine's (tel. 808/941–3338). You and a herd of about a thousand other people will be bused to a remote area near the industrial area. The beach is pleasant and so are the sunsets. The show is warm and friendly. The service can be arrogant, and the food is exactly what you'd expect when a thousand meals are served at one time.

Paradise Cove Luau (tel. 808/973–5828). Another mass-produced luau for a thousand or so. The bus takes you to a remote beach on the western side of the island. The setting is a pretty cove with palms and a glorious sunset. The pageantry is fun, even informative. The food is quite good for a luau.

Royal Luau (Royal Hawaiian Hotel, 2259 Kalakaua Ave., tel. 808/923–7311). Of the commercial luaus on Oahu, this is definitely a notch above the rest, perhaps because it's at the Royal Hawaiian. The luau happens once a week, Monday at 6, on the Ocean Terrace. With the setting sun, Diamond Head, and the enjoyable show, who cares if the luau isn't totally authentic?

Dinner Cruises

The fleet of boats gets bigger every year. Most set sail daily from Fisherman's Wharf at Kewalo Basin, just beyond Ala Moana Beach Park, and head for Diamond Head. There's usually dinner, dancing, drinks, and the setting sun. You'll find it hard to go indoors to dance—the sea and sky are just too beautiful. Dinner cruises cost approximately $40 unless noted.

Aikane Catamarans (tel. 808/522–1533). The table seating for dinner is a plus. This is one of the veteran outfits with catamarans based on an ancient Hawaiian design. Also offered: a package that takes you to the Outrigger Waikiki Hotel after the cruise to spend the rest of the evening with the Society of Seven entertainers. Fridays, there's an 8:30 rock 'n' roll cruise.

Alii Kai Catamarans (tel. 808/522–7822). Patterned after an ancient Polynesian vessel, the huge catamaran casts off from the historic Aloha Tower with 1,000 passengers. The food is good.

Hawaiian Cruises' Sunset Dinner Sail (tel. 808/947–9971). A full Polynesian revue breaks out on the high seas.

Hilton Hawaiian Village Cruise (tel. 808/949–4321). Distinctive rainbow sails carry fewer than 150 passengers to sea for a more intimate cruise than the others available.

Tradewind Charters (tel. 808/533–0220). This is a real sailing experience, and a little more expensive than the other cruises mentioned. No more than six people; champagne and hors d'oeuvres. Cost $59.

Windjammer Cruises (tel. 808/521–0036). The pride of the fleet is the 1,500-passenger *Rella Mae*, done up like a clipper ship. It was once a Hudson River excursion boat in New York. A Polynesian revue is part of the package. For an extra fee, you get "Yacht Club Service," which is dinner service in a special area, with linen and china, plus reserved seats at the revue.

Index

Personal Itinerary

Departure *Date*

Time

Transportation

Arrival *Date*   *Time*

Departure *Date*   *Time*

Transportation

Accommodations

Arrival *Date*   *Time*

Departure *Date*   *Time*

Transportation

Accommodations

Arrival *Date*   *Time*

Departure *Date*   *Time*

Transportation

Accommodations

Personal Itinerary

Arrival *Date*   *Time*

Departure *Date*   *Time*

Transportation

Accommodations

Arrival *Date*   *Time*

Departure *Date*   *Time*

Transportation

Accommodations

Arrival *Date*   *Time*

Departure *Date*   *Time*

Transportation

Accommodations

Arrival *Date*   *Time*

Departure *Date*   *Time*

Transportation

Accommodations

Personal Itinerary

Arrival *Date*   *Time*

Departure *Date*   *Time*

Transportation

Accommodations

Arrival *Date*   *Time*

Departure *Date*   *Time*

Transportation

Accommodations

Arrival *Date*   *Time*

Departure *Date*   *Time*

Transportation

Accommodations

Arrival *Date*   *Time*

Departure *Date*   *Time*

Transportation

Accommodations

Personal Itinerary

Arrival *Date*   *Time*

Departure *Date*   *Time*

Transportation

Accommodations

Arrival *Date*   *Time*

Departure *Date*   *Time*

Transportation

Accommodations

Arrival *Date*   *Time*

Departure *Date*   *Time*

Transportation

Accommodations

Arrival *Date*   *Time*

Departure *Date*   *Time*

Transportation

Accommodations

Addresses

Name	Name
Address	Address
Telephone	Telephone
Name	Name
Address	Address
Telephone	Telephone
Name	Name
Address	Address
Telephone	Telephone
Name	Name
Address	Address
Telephone	Telephone
Name	Name
Address	Address
Telephone	Telephone
Name	Name
Address	Address
Telephone	Telephone
Name	Name
Address	Address
Telephone	Telephone
Name	Name
Address	Address
Telephone	Telephone

Addresses

Name	*Name*
Address	*Address*
Telephone	*Telephone*
Name	*Name*
Address	*Address*
Telephone	*Telephone*
Name	*Name*
Address	*Address*
Telephone	*Telephone*
Name	*Name*
Address	*Address*
Telephone	*Telephone*
Name	*Name*
Address	*Address*
Telephone	*Telephone*
Name	*Name*
Address	*Address*
Telephone	*Telephone*
Name	*Name*
Address	*Address*
Telephone	*Telephone*

Notes

Notes

Fodor's Travel Guides

U.S. Guides

Alaska
Arizona
Boston
California
Cape Cod
The Carolinas & the
  Georgia Coast
The Chesapeake
  Region
Chicago
Colorado
Disney World & the
  Orlando Area

Florida
Hawaii
The Jersey Shore
Las Vegas
Los Angeles
Maui
Miami & the Keys
New England
New Mexico
New Orleans
New York City
New York City
  (Pocket Guide)

New York State
Pacific North Coast
Philadelphia
The Rockies
San Diego
San Francisco
San Francisco
  (Pocket Guide)
The South
Texas
USA
The Upper Great
  Lakes Region

Virgin Islands
Virginia & Maryland
Waikiki
Washington, D.C.

Foreign Guides

Acapulco
Amsterdam
Australia
Austria
The Bahamas
The Bahamas
  (Pocket Guide)
Baja & the Pacific
  Coast Resorts
Barbados
Belgium &
  Luxembourg
Bermuda
Brazil
Budget Europe
Canada
Canada's Atlantic
  Provinces
Cancun, Cozumel,
  Yucatan Peninsula
Caribbean
Central America
China

Eastern Europe
Egypt
Europe
Europe's Great
  Cities
France
Germany
Great Britain
Greece
The Himalayan
  Countries
Holland
Hong Kong
India
Ireland
Israel
Italy
Italy's Great Cities
Jamaica
Japan
Kenya, Tanzania,
  Seychelles
Korea

Lisbon
London
London Companion
London
  (Pocket Guide)
Madrid & Barcelona
Mexico
Mexico City
Montreal &
  Quebec City
Morocco
Munich
New Zealand
Paris
Paris (Pocket Guide)
Portugal
Puerto Rico
  (Pocket Guide)
Rio de Janeiro
Rome
Saint Martin/
  Sint Maarten
Scandinavia

Scandinavian Cities
Scotland
Singapore
South America
South Pacific
Southeast Asia
Soviet Union
Spain
Sweden
Switzerland
Sydney
Thailand
Tokyo
Toronto
Turkey
Vienna
Yugoslavia

Special-Interest Guides

Bed & Breakfast
  Guide to the Mid-
  Atlantic States

Bed & Breakfast
  Guide to New
  England
Cruises & Ports
  of Call

A Shopper's Guide
  to London
Health & Fitness
  Vacations
Shopping in Europe

Skiing in North
  America
Sunday in New York
Touring Europe